Village with a View

A Short History of Everton

Everton Village, 1818

Village with a View
ISBN 0 9525543 8 0

First Published in 1996 by Liverpool City Libraries in
conjunction with Pharaoh Press

Copyright © Liverpool City Libraries 1996

Published by
Pharaoh Press, Liverpool L3 5PE

Cover Illustration by Frank Green

Typeset, printed and bound by
𝐧𝐄𝐦𝐨
Liverpool, L3 4BD

Village with a View

A Short History
of Everton

Pharaoh
Press

Acknowledgements

Thanks are due to the following people and organisations who all helped in various ways to make this publication possible...

Lawrence Fulton, Mr and Mrs Bryan Turner, Frank Green, Miss M.S. Farr, Elizabeth Murphy, Ann Moore, Ann Cunningham and family, Bill Rickerby, Joe Palin, Alex Cowan, Hank Walters, Mr and Mrs Roberts, Miss Povah, Mr Ambrose, Christina Young, Mrs Spruce, Mrs Jackson, Mrs Fleming, Sam Crystal, Mrs Cohen, FB McCann, Mrs Florence Jones, Paulette Cluny, Frances Mason, Peter Wallace, Phil Taylor, Susan Westoby, Nemo, David Stoker and the staff of Liverpool Record Office, Janet Goodwin, Aldi, Macdonalds, Co-op Funeral Services, Everton Football Club, Liverpool University, St Domingo Tenants' Association, North Everton Neighbourhood Council, Farmers' Fare.

Researched and Compiled by
J Barrett & E Greenwood

Dedication

To Katie Flynn, with thanks for her help,
support and kindness in the production of this book

M. G. del.   H. H. sc.

THE ANCIENT FIRE-BEACON,
NEAR LIVERPOOL.

This Specimen is printed by J. M'Creery
of Liverpool, with Ink made from Corn,
burnt at the Great Fire in Liverpool,
September, 1802.

The above Engraving has been executed for the intended
History of Liverpool.

Contents

Preface

The first time I ever met Evertonians in force was when I was asked to give a talk at the Everton Library. They were a fantastic audience, but what really pleased me most was that they did as much talking as I did! And, by golly, they knew their history of Liverpool and Everton in particular. You cant fault them – you can't beat the experts!

So when Eileen Greenwood, the Everton librarian, told me she was hoping to bring out a book on old Everton, with reminiscences by Everton people, I thought it was a marvellous idea. I have to admit I didn't know whether it would work, though, but when Eileen rang me up and asked me if I would like to do some of the interviews I was really delighted. I knew I would be meeting people who would be able to tell me all the things which I most wanted to know and whose friendliness and forthcoming manner would make my task an easy one.

And this certainly proved to be the case. Lovely people with a richness of experience which I would never have guessed at, met me, talked to me ane made me welcome in their homes. The result of those interviews you can now read in this book and I hope you will enjoy reading them as much as I enjoyed listening to them. The librarians have worked extremely hard to bring out this book, particularly Eileen, and I am sure that now you can see the results of their labours you will think them as worthwhile as I do.

Everton Library has stood at the top of Mere Lane, serving the people of Everton for a hundred years. It is a real part of Everton and is, in fact, one of the few parts which remain untouched. It continues to serve the community well − long may it thrive.

Katie Flynn
October 1996

Introduction

by John Barratt

The Beginnings

The ground which was eventually to be occupied by the village of Everton originally resembled such neighbouring areas as present-day Bidston Hill – a sandstone ridge, covered with gorse and heather, and later scattered patches of cultivated ground and pasture where the few inhabitants grew their crops and grazed their livestock.

Everton is first mentioned by name in the Domesday Book of 1086, when it is called 'Hireton' – generally taken to mean 'Higher Town or settlement'. It was part of the vast estate in the North West of England granted by William the Conqueror to his cousin, Roger of Poictou, and passed through various noble and royal hands during medieval times, remaining for hundreds of years a small farming community, whose inhabitants seldom ventured further afield than the small fishing village and little port of Liverpool, at the foot of the hill on the banks of the Mersey.

The first important building to be erected in Everton was the Beacon, built in the 13th or 14th centuries on the spot now occupied by St George's Church. Commemorated by the name of Beacon Lane, the Beacon – which collapsed after a storm in 1803 – was about eight metres high, and that was the site of a signal fire which could be lit in times of emergency, such as the threat from the Spanish Armada of 1588, and formed part of a network covering the whole country.

The other principal feature of the time was a mere which was situated in the area where Mere Lane now runs, and was used to water the local cattle.

Prince Rupert and the Civil War

At the beginning of the 17th century, Everton probably had a population of no more than two to three hundred people, and had so far remained largely unaffected by outside events. But the outbreak, in 1642, of Civil War between King Charles I and his Parliament brought a rude awakening for the village.

From the spring of 1643, Liverpool had been held by the Parliamentarians, and in June of the following year, the King's nephew, Prince Rupert, arrived with a Royalist army, his

Prince Rupert

objective to capture the port and so safeguard the King's sea links with Ireland.

Prince Rupert established his main encampment on the heights of Everton, which provided an excellent observation point overlooking Liverpool, and a fairly healthy base for his troops when they were not manning the siegeworks closer to the town. It is said, that when he first looked down on Liverpool from Everton, Rupert described the little port as "a nest of crows which a parcel boy might take."

In fact, the Prince was an experienced and capable soldier, and any such comment was intended more as a morale booster for his men than a realistic assessment of the task before him.

In the event, Liverpool held out against bombardment and assault for about five days, and Rupert is reputed to have established his headquarters in a cottage, which – until it was demolished in 1845 – stood at the top of the south side of Everton Brow, although he actually stayed in Bank Hall, Kirkdale.

Two skeletons uncovered when St George's Church was being built in the early 19th century were thought to have been Royalist casualties of the siege, possible soldiers who had died of sickness or wounds. The episode was commemorated by the street names of Rupert's Lane and Rupert Hill.

Later in the year, Everton will have seen the presence of soldiers of the opposite side, when Sir John Meldrum led operations to regain Liverpool for Parliament.

18th Century Everton

With the end of the Civil War, Everton returned to its usually peaceful existence. During the 18th century it remained a small village outside the boundaries of the rapidly growing town of Liverpool. Life will have been mostly routine, with most activities centred around agricultural matters.

A number of fairs were held in the village, most notable perhaps being the Everton Cattle Fair, which was held as late as 1828, when it was noted that sheep were being sold for 35/-, lambs for 18/- and black cattle – possible bought in from North Wales – for £16.

Amusements in 18th century Everton were self-made. Among those recorded were marbles, hops and tops, and more exotic sounding games like 'foot and a half and bandy' and 'chuck-hurdles'. Among the men, wrestling, cudgeling and hurling were popular. By 1830, a chronicler wrote with rather priggish satisfaction, various "vulgar amusements" had almost ceased.

These included 'grinning through a horse collar' and eating scalding porridge! Another custom to have fallen into disuse was the traditional November 5th bonfire on Rayner Lane. For many years, the Township had given a sum of money – varying from 1/- to 3/- to the local lads to pay for the cost. However, the custom had been causing a growing nuisance, and it is recorded that in 1806 the 'bonfire lads' were actually paid not to light it! The bonfire was finally banned in 1811.

Another well-known local event until 1819 was the annual

Easter Fair held on Folly Field on the southern edge of Everton Township.

A famous Everton celebrity in the 18th century was a young woman named Molly Bushell, who lived in the village, and who struggled to support a large family. A kindly doctor suggested to her that she might increase her income by making and selling toffee, and gave her a recipe for treating coughs, colds and sore throats. The resulting concoction proved to be a great success, and Molly continued in business until her death in 1818.

As a result of Molly's success, several competitors also entered the toffee business, the best known being Cooper's Toffee Shop, started in about 1810 by Mary Cooper at N°1 Brownside. It was this establishment which became known as the Everton Toffee Shop, and eventually passed to three servants of the founder, who by 1871 had set up as the confectioners Ellan, Unsworth and Leonard at 21 Moss Street.

By the middle of the 19th century, Everton Toffee had achieved national fame, and visitors to the area took some home with them, in the same way that holiday-makers have bought seaside rock in more recent times. In the 1860's, the qualities of Everton Toffee were celebrated by a local rhyme:

> *"Everton Toffee! Ever dear to lass and lad:*
> *More certain cure than balm of Gilead.*
> *Come friends, come buy – your pennies give.*
> *While you keep sucking you'll be sure to live."*

Yates and Perry's Map of 1769 shows Everton as still only a

cluster of about thirty cottages centred around the village square, but the attractions of its position overlooking the Mersey were beginning to come to the notice of the increasingly wealthy Liverpool merchants.

One of these was George Campbell, a West Indies merchant, privateer owner and sugar refiner, and Mayor of Liverpool in 1763. He bought some land in Everton in 1751, and called it the St Domingo Estate, after a rich French prize taken off the West Indian island of that name by one of Campbell's privateers.

In 1793 the original house built there by Campbell was demolished by the new owner, John Sparling, another merchant, who erected in its place the finest mansion in Everton, St Domingo House.

Sparling, Mayor of Liverpool in 1790, had high social pretensions, and had himself an impressive tomb erected in Walton Churchyard, which could be seen clearly from the windows of St Domingo House, and was probably intended to impress future owners!

However, Sparling's successor at St Domingo House is unlikely to have been overawed by the spectacle. He was Prince William, later Duke of Gloucester, who in 1803 was appointed nominal military commander of the Liverpool district, and made his headquarters in the house. It became, for a time, a great centre of banquets and other social gatherings for Liverpool society, and the growing number of merchants and their families who were now living in Everton.

Unfortunately, Prince William fell out with local society when his name was omitted by the Mayor in the loyal toasts proposed at a banquet given for the Prince regent and the Duke of Clarence. Prince William and his officers walked out in a huff!

St Domingo House later became St Edward's College and was used as a seminary and school. It was demolished in 1938.

Another local 18th century building, used for rather different purposes, was the Bridewell or 'Round Jug', built in 1787 on a triangular piece of ground at the upper end of Everton Brow, and intended for "the temporary reception and incarceration of the unruly, the vicious and the criminal", until they could be transferred to another prison, such as Kirkdale Gaol.

As it turned out, the first people to be imprisoned in the Bridewell were th local Constable and his deputy, who were locked in by the local blacksmith whilst they were inspecting the bolts he had fitted! Eventually their cries for help were heard, and the blacksmith persuaded to release them. The story that the Bridewell had tunnels beneath it, dug by Chinese labourers to house slaves, is untrue.

Despite its rural situation, life in 18th century Everton was not always peaceful and civilised. In 1782, a lady's companion, Miss Molly Banks, who lived in a villa on Breck Road, was awakened one night by a noise. She looked out of her window to see burglars about to break in. In an early example of 'having a go', she seized a convenient musket and opened fire. The criminals made off, leaving bloodstains in the road, with the result – as the contemporary historian of Everton, Robert Syers, remarked — "Robberies were unknown in the township of Everton for a considerable time afterwards."

This was not the only thrilling episode in Everton at the turn of the century. In 1812 there had been series of attacks on hackney carriages carrying prosperous passengers out to the suburbs of Liverpool. In a carefully planned undercover operation, armed police hid in a carriage, and were ambushed by five robbers, armed with blunderbuss and pistols, in Everton Lane (now Everton Road) near where the Adam Cliffe Day Nursery now is. A furious battle followed. One constable was shot through the arm, another had cuts around the head, and a third a gash over the eye. But two of the gang were captured, and two more arrested the following day. In April 1813, three of them were found guilty and executed at Lancaster, so that Syers was able to report three years later, "since then hackney coaches have been safely permitted to ply in this district."

Another exciting event, albeit of more peaceful nature, also took place in 1812. On 12th August there was great excitement when Robert Syers, with perhaps pardonable exaggeration, wrote there occurred "an event which gave greater brilliance, activity and interest than any scene or event that had ever previously happened at Everton." Over 70,000 people had gathered to watch a balloon ascent by James Sadler, who had been the first Briton to make such a flight. Taking off from Pilgrim Villa, between Walton Lane and Sleepers Hill, Sadler had landed safely near West Derby Chapel.

'Village with a View'

Everton in 1800 was regarded as a pleasant place to live. It had a population of about 500, and was described as "a pretty village with a view, which embraces town, village, plain, pasture, river and ocean. At sunset the wonders of Everton Brow flash back the glowing radiance, showing that nothing impedes the wide prospect westwards."

In fact, Everton had become so popular that it had even taken on the role of a holiday resort! Families came to stay in the spring and summer. Among them were the De Quincey family, one of whose children, Thomas (1785-1859), was later to be best known as the author of 'Confessions of an English Opium Eater'.

The De Quinceys' visited regularly between 1801-1807, always staying at the small house of Mrs Arabella Best, in what later became Everton Terrace, which is now part of Everton Park.

For most of this period, England was involved in the long struggle against Napoleon. This probably had few effects on Everton, apart from a naval semaphore station which was erected there. The great battles and invasion scares of the war probably caused less alarm than did a proposal to build an army barracks in the village.

Many of the middle-class objected, feeling that it would lower the tone of the neighbourhood. However, or so it was claimed in a topical poem by Sylvestor Richmond, quite a few of the local females actually welcomed the prospect of the military presence!

The Ladies of Everton Hill to William Ewart Esq.

"Come forth all ye females of Everton Hill
Ne'er shall woman be wronged and her clappers lie still,
Let us tell one and all, these proud lords of creation
That we cannot submit to unjust domination.
And unless they will straightway express their contrition,
Maids, widows, and wives, all will counter petition.
A barrack, my girls, which these men think so frightful,
Is just what we want – Oh, a barrack's delightful!
We shall never stir out, be it good or bad weather,
But quite certain to meet a cockade or a feather:
And these terrible men, to our husbands' alarming,
So far from a bugbear, to us are quite charming,
I'd give him all I'm worth in the world, girls, by jingo,
For a summer night's ramble about St Domingo.
All the bands will be playing, the captain saluting,
Oh such drumming and fifing, such fiddling and fluting,
And instead of a fusty old brown coated varlet,
We shall have, at command, a smart fellow in scarlet.
What a difference, ye gods! from an ale drinking clown;
Who quart after quart each night guzzles down;
But the Captain's all life, full of life and politeness,
With a beautiful hand of exquisite whiteness."

Everton had originally been part of the parish of Walton-on-the-Hill, but its increasing popularity as a prosperous residential area resulted in a meeting being held at Halliday's Coffee House, a popular meeting place in the village, at which it was decided to collect money to build a church. Shares of £100 each were sold, and by this means, a total of £11,500 was raised. In 1813, an Act of Parliament was passed, authorising the building of a new church, to be called St George's.

The church was to be built on land provided by James Atherton, on the site of Everton Beacon, and another area was set aside for use as a cemetery. The church was to be "large enough for 950 persons, exclusive of one hundred poor persons for whom seating shall be provided." Their seats were to be marked 'Free Seats', and were "for the use of the poor of the said township of Everton for ever."

James Atherton was evidently uneasy about the prospect of dying, for it was stipulated that funerals using the cemetery must enter by the eastern gate so that they would not pass Atherton's house!

The foundation stone of St George's was laid on 19th April 1813. The church was the result of a collaboration between John Cragg, owner of the Mersey Iron Foundry, and a pioneer in the use of cast iron in building, and Thomas Rickman, a leading church architect. The result was an important new development in church architecture.

St George's had an outer stone shell, with an interior of

standardised cast iron parts assembled on site. It was the first of four 'cast iron' churches to be built in Liverpool.

Everton was now reaching the peak of its popularity as a residential area. In 1830, it was said that "Everton now abounds handsomely walled pleasure grounds and well-enclosed fields, and is conveniently intersected with admirable roads, most of them well-paved, and many of the parapets are flagged for two thirds of their breadth with admirable, well-laid strong flags."

But in fact, Everton's days a fashionable resort were now numbered. Liverpool's population was growing rapidly, and the town was spreading out towards the countryside. In 1831, Everton's population totalled 4,500. In 1835, the Township of Everton was absorbed into Liverpool.

Everton village still retained much of its traditional character, with its stone cross in the centre, and old stone cottages with mullioned windows. The houses of the merchants with their long gardens, sloped down towards Kirkdale. But the growing areas of terraced housing, built to house Liverpool's expanding population, which were appearing around Scotland Road and Great Homer Street were beginning to spread up the hill towards Everton.

Liverpool was changing rapidly with the massive influx of people from Scotland, Wales, Ireland and elsewhere. In 1847, the massive numbers of immigrants arriving from Ireland caused so much alarm that 20,000 extra special constables were appointed, and 2,000 troops stationed in Everton.

Changing Times

The building of villas and mansions in Everton had petered out by the early 1840's, with the departure of James Atherton, moving spirit in that stage of the area's development. Instead, a number of smaller houses and cottages, such as those in Albion Street and York Terrace were built.

The mid 1860's saw the great development of terraced houses in the area between Church Street and Breckfield Road. It was said at the time that this was the period "of the flight from Everton of its wealthier inhabitants, and the erection and rapid occupation of streets of small jerry-built cottages on the sites of the old mansions."

This was in fact, something of an exaggeration. Everton was never to become one of the notorious slum areas of Liverpool. But it is certainly true that the character of the place was changing as rapidly as its population was increasing. In 1851, the total stood at 25,883; ten years later it had doubled to 54,848. In 1871, it was 90,937, and it peaked in 1921 at 124,414. It is hardly surprising that such rapid expansion brought with it many problems.

In 1859 St George's School opened to help cater for the educational needs of the expanding community.

During the 1870,s, Everton was noted as a strongly Welsh community, with Welsh chapels, newspapers and with the Welsh language commonly spoken in its streets.

In 1896, another development came with the opening of the

present public library in St Domingo Road. It aroused immense enthusiasm in the local community, and it was noted that "young and old resorted to the library in such numbers that the spacious rooms provided in it were constantly crowded to excess."

Though Everton remained a warm and vibrant community for most of those living there, it was noted by the late 1930's that many of the houses often hastily built during the previous century were badly lacking in modern amenities. The work on clearing them and rebuilding, which had already begun, was to receive an unwelcome impetus during the Second World War.

Destruction and Rebirth

In common with many other areas of Liverpool and Merseyside, the Anfield and Everton districts suffered heavily in the bombing raids of 1940 and 1941.

The attacks on the Everton area began in November 1940, when the Luftwaffe dropped land mines, and continued throughout the winter and following spring. Particularly heavy damage occurred in the Anfield area in a raid on 20th December, and further destruction took place during the climax of the German raids in the 'May Blitz' of 1941.

There was heavy loss of life when the Stanley Road Co-op was hit on 7th May, and four days previously Mill Road Hospital had also been hit. The Virgil Street area of Everton was heavily damaged, and among local churches hit during the Blitz were

Our Lady Immaculate in St Domingo Road and St Augustine's, Shaw Street.

The effects of the war hastened the process of change which had already begun in Everton. By 1952, the population had already dropped sharply to 79,525, as the move out to other districts began. By the late 1960's, the often heart-rending process of tearing down the old terraced streets and replacing them with high-rise flats and more modern housing was well underway. In 1969, for example, the City Council agreed to the demolition of over 1000 of the old terraced houses. Not all of the new developments proved successful; this was particularly the case with some of the tower blocks of flats, some of which – such as the notorious 'Piggeries' – were demolished in the 1980's.

By the closing years of the 1980's, old Everton, with its close-packed streets of terraced houses rising up the hill towards St George's, had been changed beyond recognition. By 1971, as wide-open spaces once more appeared in Everton, the population had dropped to 17,623. Twenty years later, it would only be 6,310 – the biggest fall in any district of the city.

But, although the old community had vanished for ever, the long history of Everton was entering a new phase. New housing had been developed, and most striking of all, the 1990's saw the construction of the fine new Everton Park, occupying the slopes overlooking Liverpool which had witnessed so much history. Once more, Everton was 'a village with a view'.

Jimmy & Emmie Roberts and Robbo Roberts talking

Jimmy and Emmie Roberts and their son (also Jimmy, but known here as Robbo, since it's a nickname which many pals use) are all from the Everton district of Liverpool.

Jimmy: I was born in 1906 in Iliad Street, Everton and went to the Nash Grove Ragged School like my father before me. Not only was the Nash Grove a school, it was also a home for orphans built by Sir John Brocklebank. My father, who was orphaned as a lad, was brought up there and sent us to the same school. Sir John Brocklebank paid for everything – trips, everything. We used to go camping out at Bunbury, in Cheshire. It was lovely out there ... he paid.

I was the oldest of twelve children, and as the family got bigger, we had to keep moving house. We started off at Iliad Street, then went to Clifton Street, which was the next street along, then to Beresford Street, then Carson Street and we finished up in Cornwall Street – I got married from Cornwall Street.

The houses were much the same – a parlour in the front and a kitchen at the back, bedrooms on the next floor and a garret above. And a toilet in the back yard, of course, and a tap. My brother and me shared a bed, but mostly we made do with orange boxes, so my mother could have a lodger – he had the bed, of course. It helped out with the rent and so on.

I got thrown out of school when I was thirteen; someone put a mouse in the teacher's desk and the headmistress said she'd cane all of us if the guilty party wouldn't own up. She started on me – I got twenty strokes – and when my mate, who would have been next, saw it he said, "It's our kid," meaning it was his younger brother who had put the mouse in the desk. He got twelve strokes for splitting on his brother and then I gave him a good thump as well – and got expelled for it!

Having left school, my father got me a job as an apprentice wheelwright. This was in 1919 and I got eight bob* a week, which wasn't bad. I was bound apprentice for seven years, but in 1921 the firm went bust, so I went to work as a pony lad at Williamsons, the coal merchants. I got twelve shillings a week for that, and though I say 'pony lad', that was just what they called us. It was coal delivery, and the 'ponies' were dammed great horses – they needed to be strong!

I did well with the coal, I became an assistant manager first and then manager at the Knotty Ash depot. But it was very hard work and you got smothered in coal dust – we knew coal dust was good for us though, we used to chew a bit of coal as we worked – and wasn't it hard to wash off! We scrubbed under the cold water tap in our yard at the end of the day, even in winter. You'd get someone else to scrub your back.

Emmie: I remember that coal dust, the men kept saying it was healthy and they'd eat their tea with hands that were *black*, really *black*, and you'd see the white bread with all those fingermarks on...

I loved dancing as a girl – we all did. We didn't have much money, but ten of us girls would go dancing together at the Daulby Hall by the Majestic. That was when I was working at Edmonson's Sweet Works on the other side of the Majestic. There used to a be a waxworks there – it was a penny to go in and we would have tuppence; a penny for admittance and a penny to put in the musical box.

And if you waited until half-time at the Daulby Hall, you got in for threepence instead of sixpence; we didn't have much money so we usually went in at half-time. There were several floors, but we used to go upstairs, because we weren't the only ones who came in at half-time. The sailors off the Argentine boats used to come in then and we didn't like dancing with them because they didn't speak much English, so we went upstairs even though we danced pretty well.

I'd known Jimmy for a long time, but we hadn't been out together. Well, you never had any money and Jimmy didn't dance. Then he started taking me to the pictures — you could go for two bob. It cost ninepence each to get in, which left you sixpence for some sweets. I loved Sykes' licorice all-sorts, so I used to buy myself half a pound of them for the pictures, and Jimmy would get a half pound of dolly mixtures. I didn't like dolly mixtures and he didn't like all-sorts!

We got married when I was twenty-two, at St Peter's in Sackville Street, Everton, and then in 1932, we got our first pet shop — it was 1932, wasn't it? Jimmy Robbo was twelve months old; yes, it would have been 1932. It was on the Netherfield Road by the wash house, and we had another in Heyworth Street, at number 163.

Jimmy Robbo: I remember the pet shops — all of them. One was on the corner of Everton Road and then there was the one on Netherfield Road and later we opened one in Lark Lane. And we stood on the market at Birkenhead with a stall selling stuff from the shops.

We had all sorts there, day-old chicks, pigeons, monkeys, tame rabbits, and so on. We sold an awful lot of Flemish Giant rabbits. People would come in and feel their breasts and say, "I'll have that one," and you knew they were buying them for food, not for pets. It was always me who had to take them out in the back and kill them with a big stick – my father wouldn't do it, nor my mother.

Jimmy: We must have sold thousands of pigeons, thousands. People would buy them, carry them off and then come in again the next day and say, "Those pigeons you sold me – have they come back here?" The people in Everton kept the pigeons in their back yards and did an awful lot of short distance racing with them. There was the SDU – the Short Distance Union, and the NFC – the Netherfield Flying Club. I was a member of that one.

We sold a lot of day-old chicks, too. In fact we had an incubator for hatching eggs in one of our bedrooms, I got it down to quite an art. I had some old one-bar heaters and I arranged them so that the chicks got the full heat as day-olds, and were gradually moved further and further away...so they were hardened off, like you'd harden off plants before putting them in the garden.

That way, by the time they were eight weeks old you could put them straight out in the yard and they wouldn't die on you. Everyone wanted hens, you see; it was nothing in those days to see cocks and hens walking up and down the city streets, because it was a poor area and people kept them for their eggs and later, to eat. Chicken corn was very cheap, we sold it at fourteen pounds for a shilling.

We always kept our prices down in the pet shops, so people came from all over to buy from us. We bought our pet food in bulk, there was a chap who had cold storage in Rhuddlan and a shop in Rhyl and I used to collect it from there three times a week in big corrugated bins. In the end, I was sending six empty bins by rail and then going down and collecting two full bins three times a week.

Then there was a firm called Jiffy in Fazakerley, who started to tin meat for pets. This was before the war, mind you, that they started. It was expensive and no one could afford to buy a whole tin so we used to sell it for a penny a slice. They were big tins, around 14 inches by 6 inches, not like the tins you see nowadays.

Jimmy Robbo: And my father never wasted those tins. He used to cut the bottom out and solder the tins together to make the tubing for the incubator. And then there was a chap in Seaforth who used to sell whalemeat in hessian bags, so my father asked him what he did with the empty bags. "I burn 'em," he said, so my father took them and sold them to the rag and bone people for two bob each. They used them for repairing the bottoms of chairs. And of course, he bought the whalemeat for the shop.

Jimmy: That's right, you never wasted anything. During the war, the chickens still had to be fed, so I got some of the big tins and cut holes in them and put the food inside, and do you know what the food was? It was mostly breadcrumbs. There was a bakery in Derby Road and I used to take their breadcrumbs away and mix it with the biscuit waste I got from my own shops and then stir in some laying meal. My chickens did so well on it that I sold that mixture in the shop in the end.

Jimmy Robbo: One aspect we haven't touched on was that before turkeys became popular for Christmas dinner, people round here used to have a goose. They'd buy goslings off dad and fatten 'em up in the back yard all year round, and then a week before Christmas, dad and me would run round to each customer's house so's I could kill their geese. I would have been about eleven or twelve, I suppose. The people couldn't bring themselves to kill the goose they'd been feeding each day you see, so I had to do it for them.

War

Jimmy: When the war came along they said I was unfit for military service, so I joined the ambulance service – they were crying out for people. I was stationed near one of the Kirkdale Houses and we used to have to get the old folk down the air-raid shelters and some of them weren't too sure what was going on. I remember one old lady saying, "I'm not going down there, I'm going to wait for me mother," and the nurse jollying her along, telling her, "Your mother's already down there...down you go and join her." Oh, they'd get them into the shelters somehow.

I was a driver, we had first-aid men and stretcher bearers, ad we had to wait for what they called a purple warning before we started our engines up. There were strict rules about how you took people – you took the injured to hospital first and when you'd got all the injured, then you could take the dead to the mortuary. They used the old baths under Heyworth Street school as a mortuary, but we were supposed to take the bodies to Lawrence Road, by Smithdown.

Four of us were put forward for the Certificate of Bravery whilst I was there, so we got ourselves smartened up because the Area Manager was supposed to be coming down one afternoon to interview us and give us our Certificates. But he never turned up, and there we were, all smart and polished. Someone came along and told us he was coming the following day instead, which was a Wednesday, my day off. I'd arranged to go out to see the family who had been evacuated to the country, so I said I wouldn't be coming in, not me, I was going to see my family. So I never did get my certificate.

Then after a bit I went to work at Speke, building aircraft wings. That was alright, the money was quite good, but it was heavy work. After I'd been there two and a half years though, the MO sent for me and gave me a medical, then discharged me as unfit.

I went back to the pet shops for a bit and later I worked on the maintenance side for Threlfalls until they were taken over by Whitbreads. That was interesting work, I was sent round all their pubs re-painting pub signs and tackling any repair jobs which needed doing.

Jimmy Robbo: I remember being evacuated. First I was sent to Port Dinorwic for six weeks, but I came home – just in time for the May blitz. We were living on Netherfield Road at the time and the whole area was devastated and our house was badly bomb-damaged too, so dad decided to take us en-bloc to North Wales.

He knew the area because before the war, he'd done a bit of 'field work'* with a family called Boswell out Hoylake way. The Boswells were gypsies and dad had become very friendly with them. They settled at Ewloe Green during the war, so dad took us to the little village of Alltami, just outside Mold, which is nearby.

Jimmy: That's right. I got Emmie's family and my family and took the whole lot along. We had a caravan and a tent, and we bought everything up by horse and cart, camping out all the way.

Emmie: It was grand, I liked it there. I would have stayed...but we couldn't, Jimmy couldn't have lived there. We were Everton people really.

* *see glossary*

Mrs Alma Fleming

I was born in 1947 and lived at 17 Elmore Street, where I attended Heyworth Street school until I was eleven, when I went on to Lorraine Street School.

Everton was a marvellous district to grow up in. There were several churches – St George's at the top end of Heyworth Street whilst at 'our' end, St Benedict's steeple towered up in Kepler Street. And there were pubs on every comer! We also had a variety of shops and I used to go to the Co-op on Heyworth Street every Saturday for the weekly groceries – the Co-op sold everything.

There was a large Sturlas shop, too – my grandmother worked there as a cleaner, and a Maypole, two chandlers shops, one either end of Standfield Road, plenty of fruit shops and Chinese chippies and a Chinese laundry. Then there was the home made pie shop, where Mr Watts, the baker, made the most glorious pies. The queues of people waiting to be served there were always miles long! For entertainment there was the YMCA Red Triangle Club on Everton Road, where they used to hold dances for the young ones on a Saturday morning. And there was the Everton picture house where we went on Saturday afternoons to catch up on the weekly serial which they ran.

Then there was the library; we popped in there to pick up the Enid Blyton books we loved, or to look up any information needed for school exams. Then there were the Washy Baths on Netherfield Road which we used to use because our houses had no bathrooms. Heyworth Street school was very good, not only did it have its own swimming bath in the basement, it also had two drill halls. The teachers there were strict but fair: you stayed taught. Lorraine Street school was strict, too, and the headmistress, Miss Evans, was fair but firm.

We had a good childhood in Everton but I wouldn't go back there to live now, because the atmosphere isn't the same and the old neighbourhood and the community spirit has gone.

Sam Crystal's Story

Early Days

I was born in 1907, there were four boys and four girls in our family. We lived on Heyworth Street and my earliest memory is of a neighbour coming in to tell us that war had broken out. My father, who was a cabinet maker, joined the army and my mother continued to run her small shop and to bring up us children.

The shop was very small so my mother couldn't stock much. We sold mainly baby clothes, ribbons and such, overalls and pinafores, but when someone came in and wanted something we'd not got in stock, my mother would go down to the warehouse to get it. Paddy's Market, on Scotland Road, sold most types of clothing.

I went to Heyworth Street School which had a swimming pool in the basement but it wasn't safe, so we didn't use it. Instead, we were taken by the school bus to the baths in Steer Street. There wasn't mixed bathing, of course, not for children or adults. There was a day for the men and a day for the women, then. The teacher used to line us up on the edge of the baths and tell us to dive forward and do our best to keep afloat – that was how they taught us to swim! They'd fish you out with a pole if you got into trouble, but most people somehow managed to teach themselves and then we'd go to the baths of our own accord, in the holidays.

Another thing we enjoyed playing was street rounders and cricket; you played in any quiet street – there wasn't the traffic in those days, the most you saw was the milkman and his pony cart with the open cans of milk in the back and the fellows collecting the bins – and you had to keep the ball low because of putting people's windows out. It happened from time to time, but you tried to be careful. You could play in the churchyard of St George's church, but that was skipping and tops.

As soon as we were old enough we wanted to earn a bit of money...no pocket money in those days...and then we'd hang around at the bottom of any good hill until we saw someone with a handcart. If you wanted to move things in Liverpool, you hired a handcart for 6d a day, and folk were glad of a kid to give them a lift. They'd give you a penny or two. We liked the big hill by St John's Lane, near Lime Street Station. We'd do well there!

In July, when the Orange people marches, we used to hang about at the top of Havelock Street. That was a big Orange area, the Catholics mainly lived around Shaw Street. Whenever the parade passed a Catholic area they'd sound the big drum to upset the Catholics; there was a lot of bitterness then – there still is. If you wanted to get somewhere on the day of a march you'd set off early because otherwise you'd be held up. And the same at night.

They went to New Brighton by boat and at around five in the afternoon they'd be congregating to march home again. The police would be out in force to prevent trouble. The Orange people had their own church in Netherfield Road with a chap called Pastor Longbottom in charge. He was a big man, a bit like Paisley, only milder.

Work

I left school at fourteen and started work for a firm called 'Film Rent'. It was in the days of silent films and at that time the most popular film was called *The Auction of Souls* in which about a million Armenians were slaughtered. They blamed the Turks for that. I enjoyed the job alright. I was a clerk and I used to send invitations out to all the managers of the main cinemas in Liverpool, Wirral, Wallasey, North Wales and Lancashire to come to trade shows for new films.

These were viewed in the morning at 11am, at the Scala, the Futurist, the Palais de Luxe etc, and some of the managers who came controlled five or six other cinemas. When they'd seen the film the managers would book it for three or six days, if they liked it, and then they'd go down to the pub. The bosses would buy them some drinks and then the managers would sign the contract. For obvious reasons the show was usually changed twice a week.

Our office was in Manchester Street and we had a viewing room upstairs with a projector and chairs etc. When the films came back from the cinema they were run to see if there were any cracks and if so were glued up so that the cinema show could run straight on. Very interesting game, the staff got to watch most of the films.

Our room in the office was like a big safe, in case of fire – film is very inflammable, you know. The films which weren't out on hire were stored there in big round metal boxes. But of course, the talkies were coming and we weren't sure what would happen to us then, so the chap I was working with, Archie Edgars his name was, said he was going to buy a partnership in a timber business. About a week later he said to me and my pal, Jimmy McFee, that there was a job going at Woodside Lairage, so I went over and got the job of scaleman.

I started work there a week later. I went over and back by ferry – it cost tuppence – and they had a ten minute service. The lairage, which was run by the Mersey Docks & Harbour Board, were just at the top of the floating roadway so it was convenient, but I was in the offices at 3 Ferry Buildings, when I first worked there.

Gradually I went over to the lairage proper where my first job was weighing the carcasses which came in from the slaughterhouse by overhead rails. We were slaughtering almost every day so they had big cooling rooms and huge fridges and butchers came in from all over Lancashire – Nelson, Burnley, places like that. The sides of beef weighed over 300 lbs because in those days a family would have a large joint of beef for their Sunday dinner and they wanted plenty of fat on it. Today, a side weighs no more than 200 lbs because people want smaller joints without any fat on.

After I'd been on the scales for a bit I started selling offal – liver, ox-tails etc – and then I went on to lambs. As you get experience, you are taught to buy livestock, which meant moving around and was much more interesting. You had to judge the cattle live, so you had to go and see them, which meant visiting the farms on the Wirral and in North Wales.

When we bought Irish beasts we would go by train to Holyhead and the cattle floats would bring the beasts in, although sometimes they were driven on the hoof. At least a thousand sheep came over each day from Ireland, from Easter to September and the Welsh lambs came in from July to September. Most Irish cattle landed at Woodside Lairage, sheep had a separate landing lairage at Wallasey.

But it was a seven day a week job...hard work. We saw all sorts – the coolies* would come off the ships to buy mutton for the crew...they brought bales of cotton over, there was a good cotton market then.

Courting and Marriage

The first girl I took out was called Ivy Hayes, she worked in the office of the Film Rental Company. We went dancing at the Edinburgh Cafe in Lord Street, where there was a restaurant upstairs and a dance floor down below. We could have a cup of tea and a cake for a shilling, and then you could dance all you liked. Her parents kept a cafe in High Street, Birkenhead and I would take her home and then catch the midnight ferry back to Liverpool and walk all the way back to Heyworth Street.

However, the girl who was later to become my wife worked at the lairage. In those days every stall had a little office so that accounts could be paid and there weren't many girls working there at all, so of course the men used to chat them up and tell them their troubles and then ask for a date. Well, she had a few dates, some of the boys were really very keen on her, and I was beginning to be interested in girls, so one night I asked her if she'd fancy coming to a show, and she said, "No, you'll have to get in the queue!"

But I really liked her so I persevered, I tried to date her every two or three days so she'd know I was serious, and eventually she agreed to come out with me. We went for a good walk – it was a Tuesday, we finished early – and after that she came out with me several times.

We went to Raby Mere, or out to Eastham, and then one Thursday I took her to the pictures, and then it was dancing ... dancing was the thing then, and there were dozens of dance halls in Liverpool – the Grafton, the Locarno, Reeces and the Rialto in Princes Road. You could get into a dance hall for one and sixpence. After that, it went on from there.

We had a quiet wedding, but we were luckier than most, we had a house to go to. It came about because a chap I knew on the market had fallen out with his wife. He was a salesman and they used to play poker on a Friday night, hiding away in one of the fridges believe it or not, and he gambled all his money away so he had nothing left to pay the mortgage. So this chap – Alan his name was – said we could buy the house for £500 and they'd try for a council property.

It was alright; we'd saved for a bit because we were both in good jobs and although we had to watch every penny, we reckoned we could afford to buy the house. My wages were about £3 a week, but the mortgage was only £2 a month, rates were £9 a year and water rates £1.10s, so we thought we could manage. We got good bargains at the end of the day on the market, they would auction off what was left, small lambs, turkeys etc. I'd pick up a live chicken sometimes and take it home.

So food was cheap but we watched the pennies very carefully and we walked whenever we could. For instance, when we went to see my mother-in-law who lives in Kensington, we walked there to save the tram fare – it took us about three quarters of an hour each way. In fact, we walked all over the place, but Liverpool was much smaller then. It stopped at Cabbage Hall in one direction and Knotty Ash in the other, so it was compact.

There was entertainment which was free too, or as good as. You could go round the big shops – Lewis', George Henry Lee, JH Watts etc, or you could go into the State Cafe which was controlled by Joe Lyons. We would go there on a Saturday afternoon with our bowler hats and brollies, and as long as you bought a coffee you could stay and dance all afternoon. And, if you had sixpence in your pocket you could go into Maison Lyons and stay there until eleven o'clock at night so long as you bought one cup of coffee!

Then you could go to the cinema second house and come out about half-past ten – many's the time my wife and I sat in the ninepennies at the cinema and caught a late tram home. It was easier to get on a late tram because the centre of Liverpool was always very congested in the evenings, but the crowds thinned out as it got later, so the trams weren't so full.

Another thing, when I worked at the old abattoir in Trowbridge Street we used to buy a swimming contract for ten bob and that allowed us to swim in any of the Liverpool baths for a year. We went in our dinner hour and I used Margaret Street, Lister Drive and Cornwallis Street – that was grand, it was seawater.

Oh yes, there was plenty to do in Liverpool in those days. There was boxing in Pudsey Street, and you could see wrestling too, down by the old Cotton Exchange. And there were the markets – Paddy's Market was good, you would see the coolies going back to their ships, all walking in single-file and carrying the stuff they'd bought on their heads. Beer was only fivepence a pint, a newspaper was a penny and everyone helped everyone else – the poor, that is. Every road had its corner shop and you'd tell the owner if you were in trouble and everyone would give a hand. They were honest too.

Doors might be locked but everyone knew that you dangled your doorkey through the letterbox on a piece of string so you could pull it back up and get in, but people didn't take advantage. They respected property more – no one would have dreamed of setting a school alight, like they do now.

* *see glossary*

Mr Ambrose

I was born in 1929, the youngest child in a family of fourteen, though only six of us survived beyond three years old. My poor mother had lost eight children before the war, in fact two of them died of a fever within ten days of each other. So you understand that I was spoilt – so far as it was possible I got what I wanted, though our family were not well off.

Indeed my parents bought my sister a Seager piano on the never-never, which made life even more difficult, financially, but they always did everything they could for us kids. I wanted a bicycle like my brother's, but I didn't get one until the war, when he went into the army and I inherited his bike. A bike was a big thing in those days.

My father, who was a carter for Jarvises, had to work terribly hard to make enough money to bring us all up. He left home at six in the morning and was rarely home before seven in the evening, and he gave my mother £2.17.6d each week. But she couldn't quite manage, so my brother's suit went into the pawnbroker's shop on a Monday and was redeemed on a Saturday. I think my father earned around £3 a week, but he could earn an extra half a crown* by feeding and cleaning the horses on a Sunday.

When I was small I went with him, but only once − the size of those huge shire horses! They really terrified me; one false step and I could have been flattened.

We lived in Tome Street, which ran from the top of St Domingo Road down towards Netherfield Road. You passed the large stone reservoir, which was about twenty foot high, before you reached our house, number 17, which was on the opposite side of the road. It had three steps leading to the front door, a parlour which we hardly ever used, and three bedrooms − not a bad house, but not as big as the ones opposite, which had half a dozen steps up and much bigger rooms. Mr Longbottom's Protestant Reformed Church was at the bottom of the street and the only shop in the street was Cook's sweet shop.

At the back of our houses was a sort of 'court' or enclosed space common to all the houses where we boys could play football and so on. You had to be careful of windows of course, and there was one fellow, Nixon I think his name was, who must have had a grand collection of balls since he was the only person who would never return balls which crossed over into his property. You can imagine we were extra-careful near his wall!

Beside games in the 'court', we all loved the cinema, particularly the "Popular", which was on Popular Road. You climbed up a flight of stone steps from Netherfield Road and went in; posh plush seats were at the back but the front was just ordinary wooden benches. I went two or three times some weeks, and occasionally I would get a free bag of sweets – and all this for 1d to 3d for a matinee performance.

The Victoria Settlement at the bottom of Northumberland Street was another good place for youngsters. You could go there to play various games – housy-housy* was one – but it was taken over during the war and became a sort of centre where they gave out the dried milk, orange juice and codliver oil to mothers and children.

Another popular pastime was the wireless – we had a battery set which ran on accumulators and I used to be sent down to a tiny little shop by the library to change them. You handed in the used one and got your recharged one, paying the man 6d for it.

In 1940 we moved to No. 52, Tommy White's Gardens, which had shared toilets in the big gravelled square. From one of the tiny landings we could watch the lads of St Edward's College as they walked to and fro in their uniform and played the brass band. But quite soon after we moved in the college was taken over as an a Fire Service station.

We had a flat on the ground floor which we preferred since once the bombing had stared we felt safer downstairs. We hardly ever went to the shelter, but after one of our rare visits we found an incendiary had landed right outside our bedroom window!

I went to several schools in the area – Christchurch School, then the Howe Street Mission, and lastly to St George's. I well remember the day when the young man who was courting my sister came hurriedly into our home to make sure that my sister was unhurt – he told us the school and the church had been bombed. They weren't that far from us, you see. You can imagine that I had a grin from ear to ear... and indeed, we were off school for a long time, twelve to eighteen months, I think.

And when we went back we were taught for a while in private houses, with a teacher for every five or six children. Then they moved us in to the Howe Street Mission where boys and girls studied together – very unusual for those days. My last school was St George's, which I chiefly remember for the delicious white cobs which the baker delivered each break-time. They cost a halfpenny and were still warm from the oven when we got them.

Two days before the war on 1st September I was evacuated to Shrewsbury. I really enjoyed it, my adopted father took me fishing and I caught such a big fish that its tail kept popping out of the jar; they were kind people. But my mother visited me after three days – it was my birthday – and she insisted on taking me home on the 5th September. She said it was because I was wearing the same jumper that I'd left home in, but I think it was really because she missed me so much. She worked in the ROE* factory in Kirkby during the war, at first on the factory floor but then later, in the canteen.

Another game we had during the war was collecting shrapnel. It was all kinds of shapes and sizes and we used to play shrapnel ollies* with it. Someone also converted an incendiary device into a money box and hung it on the wall.

I still live in the Everton area but today it is very different. In the old days you knew all your neighbours, you chatted on the doorstep, there was always someone outside when the weather was good and you could leave your door open without fear. Regrettably, times have changed.

* *see glossary*

Mrs Pese Cohen

I was born in Liverpool in 1912 and my first memories are of 167 Heyworth Street, where my mother ran a small drapery shop during the First World War whilst my father was away in the army.

Mother and us eight children lived on the premises, of course, with a kitchenette on the ground floor behind the shop and a main room for our meals and so on. We kept the food in meat safes, or just covered over, in the yard at the back. There were no fridges then of course, nor larders and such.

Upstairs, there were bedrooms with just a bed in, nothing else. We slept three to a bed. Right at the bottom there was a cellar – my goodness, I was scared stiff of that cellar, there were spiders ... shadows ... and the candle only made the shadows worse.

We had gaslight in the living room, my mother used to burn the gas mantles before she used them, but it was candles in the cellar and upstairs in the bedrooms. We had running water –

cold, of course – but no toilet; we shared an earth closet in the back yard with several other families.

On bath-nights we had a big old tin bath in front of the open fire and it used to upset us girls because the boys were done first, which meant we had to get in their water...though it was kept hot with fresh kettles, of course. That was every Friday night. Friday night was 'Amami Night*, remember?

Very few people had bathrooms in those days, so they used the public baths. When I started work in the shop I went along to the Lister Drive baths every Wednesday afternoon – early closing day. The woman would collect your tuppence and give you a big bar of carbolic soap and run the hot water to the right depth in the tub and then leave you to wallow. My mother uses to go to the public Ritual Baths* after she'd had a baby and Jewish girls went before they were married, but it was an ordinary baths as well. That one was in Great Newton Street near the University; there's a big Jewish population round there.

My mother didn't do any washing at home, a woman from Havelock Street used to come and take it away wrapped up in a big sheet. There were an awful lot of us – ten, including my parents – and the woman had to do it the hard way with dolly pegs and a scrubbing board. She'd bring it back really clean but still wet, we'd dry it, then iron it on the old flat irons heated up on the fire.

Heyworth Street was level but all the streets running off it were steep and led down to Netherfield Road. On 12th July when the Orangemen marched, my mother used to let us go and watch, provided we stood at the top of the street and looked down the hill, in case there was trouble. It's easier to run on the flat!

There was often trouble because the men marched with drawn swords and some rode on horseback and the police stood there with batons at the ready, so it could be dangerous. I felt sorry for the children in the procession, although they probably enjoyed it – they used to march all the way down to the Pierhead and then take a boat to New Brighton.

Everton was a grand place to live in those days, it had everything; shops, places of entertainment, everything. At the bottom of Beacon Lane there was a cinema, you could get a seat for a penny at the matinees, if you hung back. First come, first served, see? You'd pay tuppence and have your choice of seats, but if you hung back you'd get what was left, so it was only a penny.

And then there was the library at the top of Mere Lane. I used to spend a lot of time there. I was a great reader, many's the afternoon I spent sitting by the fender*, reading comics, anything I could get hold of. We were friendly with the children of a general grocer which was about opposite our place, and on rainy days we used to play in their stock-room. All the food was in sacks, sugar, flour, lentils etc., and we used to squeeze our fingers into the top of the desiccated coconut sack and have a feast.

We played on the sacks, jumping from one to the other, racing around – goodness knows what the customers would have thought if they'd seen us.

There were lot of different shops in the area. Longs, a newsagent, sold sweets and papers and I can remember going there to listen to the first wireless set. There was Charles, the fishmonger, and Austen, the pork butcher. They were Germans and during the first war they had their windows smashed. We were horrified that people could do such things.

Then there was a watchmaker's in Hamilton Road, then facing Hamilton Road there was Quines, which sold everything, and in Priory Grove there was a shippon* – Gaddish's – where we went for milk straight from the cow. We took our largest jug along and the dairyman would milk the cow straight into it and we'd drink the creamy top off the milk, it never did us any harm, we were hardly ever ill.

When we were ill, though, we had a Doctor Watson who came up the stairs with his black gladstone bag to visit us. He was lovely, and though my mother could never afford to pay him he came, anyway.

There was a Chinese laundry just up the road from our shop, too – we used to take in the white damask tablecloths we used on Friday night, which was the eve of the Sabbath; the room looked lovely on the Sabbath, all white linen and scrubbed tables and candlelight. The Chinese were fantastic at their job. Those tablecloths always looked like new, and the white linen shirts for the Sabbath, they did them, as well.

The Chinamen were nice, too. One of them used to get letters from China and of course he wanted to write back, but he wrote Chinese characters so he couldn't address the envelopes. He asked our mother if we girls might address the envelopes for him if he told us what to write and she said, "Yes," so we did the envelopes whenever he asked and one day he gave us a box of chocolates – imagine that, a box of chocolates! He was a lovely little man, really generous.

Our shop didn't make us much money because the customers were local folk – hard up but good and kind – and they ran up credit so my mother lost money, she never was a businesswoman. They would pay one day but then take enough for the next, as well. In some of the slum areas conditions were terrible and of course the husbands used to drink and some of the women were as bad.

When I was working we used to stand in the doorway of the shop when the pubs were closing – at ten o'clock, in those days – and the woman would come out, in their black shawls and huge black skirts, and they'd start fighting. They'd pull each other's hair out and shout and yell...they were tough! When I was working on Great Homer Street we'd see the shawlies* come in for a new skirt and they'd put it on over perhaps half a dozen old ones they wanted another skirt, not a replacement...they wanted the warmth, I suppose.

I often remember Clayton Square in town. That was where all the flower sellers sat amongst their flowers, with their big clean aprons over their not-so-clean skirts, and their cash bags stowed away amongst their petticoats!

It was a hard life for us, though. When the war was over my father worked as a cabinet maker, a six day week, from very early in the morning until late at night, whilst my mother worked in the shop. We had to watch every penny. During the war we mostly lived on fish, potatoes and bread. Mother would buy a stone of fish from Charles the Fishmonger over the road, clean and gut it – it was mostly plaice – and then cook it along with potatoes, which we would buy by the sack. Sometimes we had a chicken, a great treat, it was always boiled so we had the soup, too.

After tea we used to go down to Brunswick Road where all the shops stayed open late, and Thomas', the greengrocer, would sell off their fruit cheap. Once we got a big bunch of bananas for a shilling. Everyone we knew did it. People left their shopping as late as they could because it got cheaper and cheaper.

My father did everything he could to save money; he cut our hair, repaired all our shoes, and even built his own crystal set. My mother was the same. She made her own bread and then we took the loaves to the bakery on the corner of Mission Place and he baked them nicely for a penny. Apart from the bread, mother did all the cooking on our old black range.

The only real pleasure my father had was going to football matches. When there was a match on you could look out of the shop doorway and you'd see nothing but people, the street was black with men making their way to the football ground. They walked, of course, and there wasn't the money for bright clothing, so the men wore mostly black and brown. And you'd know when the match was over because the street would be black again; that was the men's enjoyment of a Saturday afternoon.

It was different for kids, of course. The boys went swimming — there was a swimming pool in the basement of our school — but my mother wouldn't let the girls go. She said we'd get our deaths, but she let the boys go. As for playing out, my mother didn't like us girls — there were four of us — to play in the street so we used to go along to the Iron Church — that's St George's — and play in the churchyard until tea was ready. There was an old man who used to sit on a seat, watching us, he'd tell us when it was time for tea, because we didn't have watches, of course.

We played hoop, we spun tops with a whip and we did french knitting. Our father made most of our toys, being a cabinet maker, but the french knitting we did for ourselves — you improvised a lot in those days. You knocked four nails into a cotton reel and then you bought rainbow wool — it was cheap — and pulled the knitting through the hole in the cotton reel. We did a lot of that, and reading.

And then my father used to take us, two at a time, to the Hippodrome, up on Brougham Terrace, where the Registry Office is. We queued for hours to get into the gods. They were the old time music halls, and the shows were marvellous. We walked there and back as a matter of course, in our black stockings and elastic-sided boots!

Talking of clothes puts me in mind of the pawnbrokers. Wages were terrible, an old person's pension was ten bob a week and a man wouldn't earn that much more for a full-time job — what could you do with that? So there were pawnbrokers on every corner. On Monday your decent stuff would go in and it would come out on Friday, ready for the Sabbath.

Derek Guyler had a pawnbroker's shop at the top of Moss Street, where the Prince of Wales Hotel is; he was the father of the comedian of the same name. The pawnbrokers were a bit like moneylenders and they provided a service which was much needed. They didn't let anyone starve, they were a blessing for people in dire straits.

A working girl

One day my father said his sister had opened a new shop in Tunnel Road and had a job for me. I didn't want to leave school but we needed the money so I went and worked for my aunt and got eight shillings a week. I had to clean the windows — imagine, a little girl perched on a step-ladder out on the pavement — and serve in the shop, of course. It was a gents' outfitters.

My uncle had a Daimler and it was fantastic for me to get a lift home, I revelled in it. But the hours I put in — Sundays, too. A seven day week, though I got a half-day on Wednesdays, and we had to work late at night as well. Then I asked for a rise. My aunt said, "No, you should be grateful to be in work," so I left.

My next job was in Great Homer Street, the people were wonderful, one customer brought me a little cake every day. The boss sat in a little cash office – it was another drapery shop – and he handled all the money, but there again it was terribly long hours. It was a rough neighbourhood, but I was getting fifteen shillings a week and the shops on Great Homer Street were wonderful, often you could get things very cheaply. I went home at night by tram – it was a penny upstairs out in the open and tuppence to sit inside. As kids we always went on top, but it wasn't so good in winter.

I moved from there to Woolworths, where Taskers is now. I was in charge of toiletries and at Christmas you were expected to work until midnight stocking shelves, etc. Terribly long hours again and you were on your feet all day, though the money was slowly getting better. And of course I was growing up and I was crazy about dancing, mad about it.

We used to go to the Rialto, which was the place in those days, and the Edinburgh, which used to be underneath where the British Home Stores is now. They used to call it 'dancing under the stairs'.

On our half-day we would go to The State in Dale Street for their tea-dance. We'd all rush to sit at a table near the edge of the floor because that way you got dances, and then you'd get a date for the evening. One of the best dances was at the Pico, in the New Brighton Tower Ballroom. We went by boat, it cost about sixpence, and that was where you met young men. We had soft drinks — the boys couldn't afford alcohol — and we never worried about coming home, it was safe to walk and we were used to it.

Another thing we did was to go to Bert Vaughan's Dancing Academy in Prescot Road. We were all very good dancers. My eldest sister wasn't allowed to come gadding with us, she had to stay at home and help my mother, but then one day she went all on her own to the Palais de Luxe cinema and met a lovely tall gentleman, a commercial traveller. And later they got married — wasn't that romantic?

All us girls used to go to the Isle of Man for a week's holiday because that was another place where you would meet the boys. You would go by steerage* from Liverpool for 12/6d return and stay in cheap boarding houses and you'd have a wonderful time — all we thought about was dancing, and meeting the boys. Some of them smoked — that was sophisticated — but we made a good time out of nothing.

We had a three day holiday in the spring as well, and when the Grand National was run on a Friday, one person was chosen from each department at work to see the race. I was chosen once, we went by coach, it was fantastic. But we had to go back to work afterwards!

I met my husband at a wedding where we were both guests — a mutual friend introduced us. I was wearing a black velvet dress with a lovely rose on the shoulder and I felt the bees knees. The first thing I said to him was, "Do you dance?" and when he said, "No, I don't," I said, "Well, you're no use to me, then!" He went home and told his mother and she advised him to learn. We married...but that's another story!

* see glossary

Mrs Ashcroft
& Mrs Jackson

Mrs Ashcroft: Before the war, 12th July was one of the most eventful days of the year. We would decorate the streets with coloured paper, put flowers around the doors and windows and string bunting right across the street. Competition was keen, especially Robsart Street (where I lived) and China Street off Netherfield Road. The prize was a banner. People would come from miles to see those streets and the organised parades.

In the 1920's and 30's people would sit on the steps and play the accordion or the mouth-organ. They would make their own amusement. During the summer, fathers would help their sons make steering carts in the streets from planks of wood and pram wheels. In the winter, it would be sledges because the streets were so steep. It was good fun!

Parents would play with their children right outside their own front doors; hopscotch, skipping, football in the winter and cricket or rounders in the summer. On Bonfire Night every street would have at least two or three fires in the middle of the road. Of course, all this was only possible without the motor car.

In the 1960's, we were all gutted when the corporation told us all the houses had to come down.

Mrs Jackson: I remember the 'Foo Foo Bands' that sprang up after the war − brightly coloured clowns with baggy trousers playing wind instruments. They made a unique sound. People would give them a few coppers for their efforts, because it brightened up the day!

I also remember a children's roundabout set inside a cage on a cart drawn by an old cart horse. "One penny a ride" came the shout and all the kids would dash out. It could only get halfway up Seacombe Street (where I lived) because it was too steep for the poor old horse!

I remember my late husband, Bob, mentioning a horse and cart that used to deliver molasses on tap before the war. The 'treacle butties' were a real treat for the children!

St Domingo House

Skating in the street at St Domingo in 1840

The Weighing Machine in 1904

Everton Valley, November 1904

Netherfield Road, July 1913

The library proved very popular with young and old alike

Everyday life in and around Netherfield Road in 1927

Everton Brow, June 1927

Prince Edwin Street, July 1920

Prince Edwin Street court houses, March 1924

Mere Lane, May 1927

The hustle and bustle of Prince Edwin Street, September 1920

Everton Brow, June 1927

Everton Brow, June 1927

Mere Lane, with its busy streets and popular picture house, 1937

Everton Brow, with its famous Toffee Shop

Everton Terrace, 1931

The junction of Everton Road and West Derby Road, opposite
Grant Gardens, June 1937

The Juvenile Department at the library

St George's Church

Netherfield Road, 1950

These houses in Cobden Street, pictured above in March 1960, look in good condition, but being in the House Clearance Area they had to go, along with the Bear's Head on the corner (below)

St Ambrose Church in Prince Edwin Street
built in 1870 and demolished in 1961

A view of Everton looking north from the top of new flats
in Conway Street, 1965

Everton Heights – The Braddocks – in 1959

Miss Povah

I was born in 1915 in a rented house on Dido Street, Everton, opposite the methodist church. Our house was a two-up, two down, and needless to say we didn't have an indoor toilet; ours was in the yard at the back.

Like everyone else at that time we used gas mantles for light and coal fires for warmth, with a boiler in the back kitchen, and we took our baths in a tin tub in front of the fire.

There were six in our family, though the two eldest had left home by the time the younger ones came along. My eldest sister was a private children's nurse in a family home. She wore uniform and had a headdress rather similar to a nun's. She always cut my hair and knitted jumpers for me, but most of my clothes came from TJ. Hughes, so I rarely wore hand-me-downs.

My father worked at Bibby's as a shift-worker, doing two day shifts and a night one so though we didn't have much money we weren't as badly off as some. When my father was on a day shift he used to pass the school playground and if he saw me at playtime he would call me over and give me one of the sandwiches he took for his lunch.

I went to St Benedict's school at the top of Rupert Lane with my best friend, Jenny. The nit lady, as we called the nurse, came to the school from time to time and my mother was determined that my hair would be clean so she regularly went through it with a fine-tooth comb.

Out of school I played with dolls and bowled a hoop, and for outings, my mother used to take us, and some of our friends from the street, to New Brighton. We took our tea and the older children would be sent for hot water and for the teapot, which we had to buy. My father would join us halfway through the outing, have something to eat and then go for a drink in a nearby pub.

The families who lived around us were mostly in work and had just enough money to live on, but there was a good neighbourly spirit. We all shopped locally, at the Co-op on the corner, at Pegrams at the end of Breck Road (you could get anything there!) and at the butcher's and greengrocer's. There was also a toffee shop in Village Street which I visited whenever I could, though I never had pocket money, as such.

And it wasn't just shops which were handy, our entertainment was local, too. There was a dance hall, the Hippodrome theatre and the Lytton cinema where a child could see the show for a penny.

From St Benedict's I went on to Steer Street school and after I left, I worked at the Bake house in Whitefield Road. I had always attended church regularly and took over the Everton Road Methodist Church Brownie pack, taking them on outings in the summer. After church a group of us girls would go for a walk and then for a cup of tea at someone's house, taking it in turns. We had Christian Endeavour concerts and a Christmas Fair at the church and I helped with both of these.

During the war I worked in the automatic telephone service. I travelled to work by tram – the trams went along the bottom of the street from Clubmoor to town – and because the others had joined the services, this left just my father and myself in the house, my mother having died. We had an air raid shelter in the street but it was never hit.

After the war I remember the May Day procession held at the Methodist church. A young girl would be May Queen and would be taken around the streets in a carriage.

In 1968 the Dido Street houses (and most of the area) were demolished. The only thing that had changed in our house was that by the time I left, the houses were all on mains electric, otherwise they were just the same.

Bill Rickerby, Joe Palin and Alec Cowan talking

Schooldays

Liverpool teemed with schools because it was such a heavily populated area and the boys had their own ideas about each one. Everton Terrace School – which none of them attended – had a two-tiered school yard and hot showers, whilst Heyworth Street school had a swimming bath fifteen foot long and three foot deep – the first school in the city to have such a thing. The Heyworth Street headmaster in Bill's time was a man called Solly Emlyn from Southport.

Joe, on the other hand, who was born in Jefferson Street, went to St Benedict's school in Kepler Street. Joe thought the church schools had limited playgrounds because the Kepler Street school had a small play area, whereas Heyworth Street playground was large. After that he went to St Margaret's on the corner of Belmont Road, Anfield.

Alec went to St Judes, in Holborn Street.

The boys were all streetwise and knew the best places to play. Alec played in Grant Gardens, at the end of Everton Road, where there had once been a cemetery and there was an old necropolis. It was a quiet and pleasant place, though there was a band there on Sunday afternoons with benches for the older people to sit on.

But streets were the best playgrounds. You could play football, though the streets were narrow and it was liable to cause accidents. Joe remembers the cry going out "Pay for your own china, pay for your own china!" which meant if you break the window glass you pay for it yourself.

Talking about windows coming out reminded Joe of bonfire nights when the huge bonfires, lovingly piled higher and higher by the kids, would be so hot when they were set alight that paintwork would blister and windows would crack Joe said he'd seen windows go in while the woman of the house was shopping and – there was always a handyman in every street in those days – someone would nip round to the Everton Glassworks, slip in the house, put the new window in, and the woman was none the wiser.

There were plenty of games which could be played in the street. Kites – usually homemade – would be flown, marbles would come *in and everyone would have a craze for them, and then there were cherry-wobs*, which were much-prized and absolutely free of course...*

Joe: The kids would originate their own cherry wob schools. They would sit with their backs against the wall and make a little pile of cherry stones on the pavement in front of them, and kids passing by would have a go to see if they could knock the sitter's stones and win some for themselves. But if you tried, and missed, the sitter took your stones. And there were cigarette cards, of course. You'd have a stall for swops... everyone had cigarette cards.

Then there was Euialio*, or Relievio*, we called it both. You'd have two teams, one team would stay behind and the other team would hide. It astonishes me now that instead of hiding somewhere good — there were all those back entries and little streets — we used to go to the same old hiding places and the other team would know exactly where to find us.

So anyway, then you'd be found and caught and taken back to the wall which was the other team's 'gaol', and one boy would guard them. Now the people in gaol could be released as it were, if one of their mates who hadn't been found could get to them, without being caught, and they could escape. And of course when you were in gaol you would shout "Euialio!" or "Relievio!" until someone came.

Bill: And there was pitch and toss, though that was mostly for men; men played that mostly because it was gambling. They crouched on the pavement, the players, and it was nearest the wall, or two head or two tails, they were the ones that won and took the money. The fellers were mostly out of work, it was something to do. It was their housekeeping money. They had lookouts, because it was gambling, see? The notice would stop it if they caught you.

Alec: We used to collect jamjars and all, and take them back to the rag and bone shop. If it was a 2 lb pot you got a penny, but if it was only a 1 lb one you'd get a halfpenny. Then you could go to the Saturday matinee at Lyttons cinema. And it wasn't just jamjars, you could take sauce bottles back to the Paragon Pickled Onion Factory on Everton Road, on the corner of Lytton Road – you only needed to take in four and that would be your money for the pictures.

And Edmondson's Lemonade factory on Guildford Street would pay for bottles, too. You went down Lytton Street and turned right along Breck Street and the factory was there. The bottles had the flip top or the marbles that you pressed down with your thumb and they wanted them back.

Then there was the rag and bone man. You took your rags in and he weighed them on the scales and told you how much he'd pay, and if the rags were wet they were heavier so you got more money. And there was the scrap metal yard along by the Salvation Army place in Breck Road – Baines Place. They paid anyone who took in bits of metal.

You could run messages for neighbours, too. You'd go to the

shop for a loaf, or to the dairy for half a pint of milk. And you never had to hold your hand out.

Of course, being Everton, football was a craze whether you played in the street or watched your team.

Bill: The first thing I remember clearly was my uncle giving me sixpence – that was a lot of money in those days – to go and watch Everton play and get myself some sweets when I got there. I was six or seven, I suppose. There was a boys' pen at Everton. it was a closed one – there were no other closed pens in Liverpool then. Liverpool was open, by the paddock, because some years later, in 1933, I nearly got killed there. Everton was beaten 7-4 by Liverpool and a lot of the men came in over the top, I was lucky to get out alive. Incidentally, I called the fellow my uncle, but he wasn't related to me at all. He was Sandon the butcher, I just used to call him uncle. He took over the shop from my grandmother, who had it during the first world war, it was next door to Peter Gannicliffe, the barber who had a hare-lip – you couldn't always understand what he said.

There was a ladies hairdresser at the back. He started out, did Gannicliffe, at 53 Heyworth Street but later he moved over the road between Taylor's bread shop on the comer of Eastlake Street and Foley's, the sweet shop. He was a popular barber; on a Saturday you couldn't get through the door for fellows getting shaves, haircuts and so on. Yes, we looked after ourselves in those days.

Money was short, but it went a long way. For sixpence you

could get a glass of mild, five woodbines and a box of matches, and still have a penny change.

Alec: When I was a kid we used to get given a penny by someone and they'd say "don't spend it all in the one shop!" And you'd go round and buy a farthing's worth of dolly mixtures, the same of aniseed balls, then you'd go up to Higgets on West Derby Road and get some mint drops. After they moved from Mill Road they went to the top of Heyworth Street, then up by the Palladium.

And there was toffee ... Mother Nobblets sweet shop in Village Street made the best toffees, the ones they used to give away at the football matches. Taylor's, Sykes and Scotts were all the main bakery shops and there was a dairy by the Savoy. Griddles came round with a molasses cart pulled by a pony and they'd sell it to the kids - a great treat. Haywood the herbalist was at N° 11 or 13 – he had a sort of milk bar.

Health and Hygiene

Health must have been a great worry for everyone, because a doctor's visit was expensive. Dr Richmond was a Labour councillor as well as a doctor and he would treat the men who were out of work and their families free, or for whatever they could manage, while other doctors wouldn't come over the doorstep until they'd seen the colour of the patient's money. But there were clinics, and some of the doctors were well-liked...

Bill: There were some good doctors, though. Popular. There was Dr Dixon and Dr Strelitz in Shaw Street, the queue would be fifty or sixty deep of an evening, and you used to have to pay four bob a visit just after the second war, and that was a lot of money. At one time I remember having to visit three times in a day – that was twelve bob... that's a lot of money!

Alec: There was a school clinic on Everton Road on the corner of Plumpton Street, and on the other side was Mill Road, where we saw the dentist. They'd come round the schools and look in your mouth and they'd say "dentist on such-and-such a day," and you went, you didn't have any choice.

The dental clinic was all right but the Plumpton Street Clinic was very unhygienic, they never washed the blankets or anything like that, so of course infections got passed on. In fact the writing was on the wall for Plumpton Street clinic after the scabies epidemic – we had to have baths, then, and they painted us with gentian violet*.

Joe: I can tell you a story about that clinic. I had a younger brother, Arthur, and he had dreadful impetigo all over his face. It's an awful story, this. He was sent to Plumpton Street for treatment, and while he was there he contracted some ailment – II can't remember what – and he was put in hospital out at at Fazakerley.

Well, he got over the first ailment but then he contracted something else, and in time he got over that, too. This all happened in hospital, remember. Then he got whooping cough and whilst he was still in hospital recovering from that he contracted poliomyelitis and that's why he had to wear callipers on both legs.

Bill: I remember the Hannah family in Stonewall Street; number thirty-three I think it was. There were the parents and four kids and within a fortnight the father and three of the kids had all died from diphtheria. We had knockers-up in those days. He used to come along with a pole and bang on the windows... instead of an alarm clock. And he and three of his kids all died.

Then there was the Hahnerman Clinic – that was in Hope Street and adults could go there too. You paid a penny to get a tally and then you saw a doctor. That was in the late 'twenties. early 'thirties. Then there was the nit-nurse. they came round the schools and if you had nits they sent you to the clinic.

Joe: Yes. we all remember the nit nurse. They'd come round and then you'd see some kids – the girls were more noticeable of course without any hair at all because they'd gone to the clinic and had it all cut off. That was when their heads were really full of lice. It was hard to keep clean because the housing was really bad and almost no one had bathrooms or hot water.

Bill: Yes, and in the courts – they were terrible, them – all the people in all the houses shared a toilet at one end of the court. But we had backyard toilets. one per house. Generally speaking they were better class houses once you came up off Netherfield Road. Across Heyworth Street to Stanfield Road they were better, bigger rooms, higher ceilings. But from Netherfield Road down to the docks there was poor housing down there. I'm not saying they were slums because a lot of them took a great pride in keeping their homes nice, but they were second rate houses really.

Alec: Oh yes, I've heard it said that they scrubbed their steps Saturday night and Sunday morning no matter what.

Bill: When you think, it's surprising there weren't more illnesses. My uncle was a butcher and he didn't have a fridge, he just used to cover the meat up as best he could, and on a Saturday night in Kepler Street there was a place where you could get a handcart for a few pence – a float one or a stiff one.

Dad and myself used to get a handcart and collect the meat which hadn't sold from my uncle's shop to take it to the cold storage in Daulby Street and then we'd take the neck-ends round all the lodging houses in Lytton Street and Everton Brow – that was Dad's bunce when he was out of work. They liked the neckends and such to make soup. and used the meat, too, of course. Come to that, there was always someone selling joints of meat round the pubs on Great Homer Street and I daresay they weren't too fresh.

There were Corporation Baths in Netherfield Road, in Heyworth Street where the laundry is now – I liked those there was bags of life there. There were also baths in Margaret Street, Cornwallis Street and Westminster Road – they also had salt water swimming baths there.

Neighbourliness

Bill: There was a woman in the Penrose Street who had triplets in 1930 – it was in all the papers, the *Express* and the *Echo*. Photographs, the lot. And she thought it was God's punishment, having triplets, because there was no sort of assistance in those days if you had a multiple birth. But once they were born neighbours came up the back entry and through the yard and into her kitchen. They brought her anything they could afford and they took all her dirty washing back home, did it and returned it clean and ironed.

That was how she managed with those three babies – with help from the people around her.

Alec: Don't forget the soup kitchens, during the Depression. There was one behind Brougham Terrace – you'd get a big chunk of bread and a bowl of hot soup. Free, of course.

Bill: And then there was the Everton Road Methodist church. If you went there four Sundays in a row you'd get a ticket and kids could go and get a free breakfast on Christmas Day.

Working days

Work was hard to get and harder to keep and wages were very low. The hours were long and what was most valued was not a bit more money but a promise of regular employment. You could open a shop – a lot of people did – but most people lived from hand to mouth, scraping by, because you had to give credit to those customers who asked for it and though folk paid when they could, it wasn't always possible...

Alec: The best jobs were postman, policeman or something with the Corporation. Dockers were either taken on or not, it all depended how fast they could run between docks, so there was no security there.

Bill: Or if a docker had a half-crown he'd make a slit in an apple and give the apple to the foreman. That might get him a job. But it might mean you'd work all day for nothing.

Shops didn't make you a fortune, either. My grandmother had a sweetshop in Heyworth Street and she said that the overheads were too heavy so she let my father have half the shop to do his cobbling*. But the fellow next door used to do a bit of snobbing* as well, which caused friction between them, and in the end my father gave it up. He'd been shell-shocked in the first war and it made him slow – very good and careful, but slow. Then he went chimney-sweeping. He was well-known all over for chimney sweeping. He had to start work at three o'clock in the morning and when he came home he was filthy; he had a bath in the kitchen and it was my job to wash his back.

Then in the afternoons he sold ice cream around the streets. He used to make the ice cream himself, in our yard.

Joe: My grandmother had a butcher's shop from around 1870 and they made a very good thing of it. When she died, in 1941, and the will was read she left a lot of money – around £20,000 –

but I think they were luckier than some. You see she was a farmer's daughter and my grandfather was a butcher's son, and I imagine that he went out to the farm to buy beef or lambs, and met her. And then they didn't just have the shop in Brunswick Road, they had another in Prescot Street, and the yard there was used as a slaughter house for beasts he'd bought.

Bill: My dad was one of only two first-aiders in the area in the thirties, he was trained by the St John Ambulance people, and he was called out regularly, every time there was an accident. One interesting one comes to mind. There's a bend in Heyworth Street with a pub on the comer – that's the Elephant, on the comer of Stonewall Street.

In the early thirties there were always accidents on that comer, because cars we becoming more commonplace. One Bank Holiday a motorcyclist was coming along Heyworth Street and he didn't make the bend, he shot straight through the door of the pub and ended up on the counter. They didn't serve him, mind. They took him to hospital, but no one else was hurt because no one was standing near the door when he came through it. Strange, that – on a Bank Holiday and all!

Course, I say they took him to hospital. but there weren't any ambulances. You went down to the old box on the comer. There was a phone in it and you pulled the handle and got put through to the police. No one else, just the police. And they dealt with it then.

He went round the theatres too, with the St John's Ambulance.

One time, Anna May Wong sprained her ankle and he had the pleasure of seeing to her. She was a famous actress in those days. And he saw to Dixie Dean when he played baseball – there was a baseball league in Liverpool in the thirties – they put celebrities on to draw the crowds.

* see glossary

Growing up in Everton
Christina Young

I could scarcely contain my excitement. After weeks of asking "How long now Mummy?" the great day had arrived, My first day at school! I wore new hand-knitted leggings under my coat and a 'pixie' bonnet tied under my chin as my Mother and I stepped out of our front gate into Newlands Street that frosty January morning in 1953.

The trams clattered past and the gas lamp at the end of Breck Grove still flickered as we made our way along Queens Road to Whitefield Road and the school I was to attend for the next four years, The distant hum of noise increased to a crescendo as we neared the packed sweet shop where they sold penny sherbet dabs and four-a-penny sweet cigarettes.

Rounding the corner I saw the school loom into view and more children than I had ever imagined existed were pouring through the gates and into the playground. I could not understand why some hung back crying and clinging to their mothers as if reluctant to join this noisy, happy throng.

There were sixty of us in class one. We each had a slate to write on and copied the letters that Miss May – our teacher – wrote on a huge blackboard. Mid-morning we were each given a small bottle of milk and a straw. We took turns to paint, play in the sand pit or 'Wendy House' and all listened attentively to Miss May's daily 'story'. There were books too, 'Janet & John', 'Noddy' and 'Milly Molly Mandy' soon became part of my life.

The following year our teacher announced a class trip to join the local library – the 'Rawdon' in Breck Road. My home boasted several bookcases full of books but here there were thousands lining the walls and we could choose any of them. Books – especially adventure stories – became a central part of my life. I soon realised they were a wonderful means of escape.

It was not easy being an only child of strict elderly parents (my mother was 47 and my father 69 when I was born). Absorbed in a story book I could pretend to be one of the characters – usually a child of a big happy family – searching for buried treasure or secret tunnels. The area around Newlands Street offered plenty of scope for the imagination.

There were bommies (bombed sites) with unexplored corners and partly collapsed walls, and as the government 'slum clearance programme' got under-way, an increasing number of derelict houses too. Their dank, musty cellars aroused the curiosity of local children – especially during the long summer holidays when games of skipping, ollies*, top & whip and even off-ground tick and 'Il-ally-o'* had become boring and there were no more tar-bubbles to burst in the sun-drenched roads.

Sometimes we made our way to the playground adjacent to the bowling green on top of the water-works in Aubrey Street or the newly renovated Grant Gardens which had a wonderful variety of swings, slides, roundabouts and monkey bars.

On Sundays I was not allowed to play at all and the only books I was allowed to read were religious ones and the Bible, My Father had co-founded Bethesda Church (now Bethshan) in Breckfield Road North many years previously and three times each Sunday I attended the services with my parents. I could never understand why the preacher found it necessary to jump around in the pulpit shouting at us all. Later we left there and went to Fabius Chapel in Everton Road which was run by friends of my Mother's.

My Father also attended Stanley Park Church in Fountains Road. He took me to see my first film there (I was never allowed to go to the cinema. It was called 'Martin Luther'. The church was packed as everyone sang "Dare to be a Daniel" with great gusto. I felt hot and sticky but my Father would not let me remove my bonnet as he said the Bible stated women must keep their head covered in church as a sign of respect. I was six years old!

In 1957 I left Whitefield Road school. I had been off school ill for three months with something my mother referred to in hushed tones as 'bad nerves'. Dr Goodman, from his surgery in a large house in Queens Road had prescribed a continuous supply of pills and a change of school had been recommended.

I found Anfield Road Juniors very different from Whitefield Road school. The main objective of the teachers seemed to be to shunt as many of their pupils as possible into grammar schools via the eleven plus. However, I rebelled and stated I wanted to go to a secondary modern school with my friends.

1 went to Steers Street – Prince Rupert Secondary Modern School for Girls – along with my best friend Carol. Carol and her brothers also went to Murray Hall Mission on the corner of Poplar St and Breck Road. She invited me to the Sunday School with her. Some of the happiest times of my life were spent at the Mission. Everyone was so light-hearted and full of fun.

On Sunday School anniversaries a band led us all through the streets with our banners proudly displayed and singing our favourite hymns. There were Christmas parties and games – and no-one insisted the girls wore hats in church!

Sometimes we joined up with St. Domingo Mission. Meanwhile I had discovered another library!

A classmate was seriously into 'Biggles' books – which she claimed were even better than the 'Famous Five'! St. Domingo library had loads of them!

I became a regular member for several years. I usually went on Saturdays, sometimes calling to see my Auntie Cissie in Priory St on the way. Auntie Cissie Oliphant − my Father's eldest sister, had been a music hall singer in Liverpool in the early part of the century and had many exciting tales to tell. Sometimes on my way home I wondered through the nearby streets.

During the war my Mother − then May Johnson − had been the Minister in charge of Beacon Lane Mission, She had hoped to be a missionary in Brazil but ill health prevented it and having gained a Diploma In Theology she came to Liverpool instead to live at the missionary home belonging to the 'Sudan Interior Mission' in Oakfields.

In 1967 after my Father's death and the demolition of Newlands Street Mum and I moved to Saker Street near Stanley Park. Lots of her old congregation still remembered her and welcomed her back to the area as Miss Johnson of Beacon Lane Mission. Much to Mum's dismay − and my amusement − I became known as Miss Johnson's daughter.

The years passed and I used the Central Library and their books, no longer as a means of escape from reality but in my studies for the O and A-levels I had not taken as a teenager and later an Open University degree. In recent years I became aware that the libraries were extending their role and services to encourage and promote community-based activities. I have attended writers workshops, discussion groups and committee meetings in a variety of their community rooms. Most importantly, for me, the friendly, helpful staff in libraries throughout Liverpool regularly display the posters for Mental Health Awareness Days that I organize each year in Central Library.

Over forty years on from my first introduction to the libraries whilst growing up in Everton, they are still a very important part of my life and I feel sure will always remain so.

* *see glossary*

Ralph Walters Talking

I was the eldest child in our family and was born on 2nd August 1933 in the Mill Road Maternity Hospital. My mother, Emma, was in the wash house down in Everton Valley when her pains started, so she got the other women to look after her washing and went home to 25 Stirling Street. Then she got the number 33 tram car through to Breck Road, getting off at the Old Royal Picture House. She walked through to the maternity hospital from there and I was born three hours later.

We lived at number 25 whilst I was very small but then moved to 31 Severn Street, which was a two up, two down with rent at two shillings a week. We had an outside toilet in the small back yard – it was freezing cold, going out there in winter time.

The back kitchen had a big iron boiler for clothes etc., but we never used it for washing, we used it for live bait! My Dad was a keen fisherman and would bring eels home and put them in the boiler and then use them as bait. My dad did well with fishing, he used to make lay lines with horse-hair, bait them with lob worms and then lay them out on the beach so when the tide came in the fish would follow and take the bait.

We caught all sorts, flukes, sole, plaice, mud dabs, all sorts. Now one day my mum was cleaning our catch in the back kitchen and Dad came in. He always washed his own socks, didn't trust my mother to do it right, and he had just poured a basin of water and set out the soap powder on the draining board when someone came to the door.

Mum finished cleaning the fish and came over to the draining board to roll them in the flour she had put out ready. She popped them into the frying pan and noticed that the fat was all frothy, but it fried the fish all right so she popped them onto a couple of plates and added a pile of lovely golden chips and some baked beans.

We started to eat and Dad sprinkled his fish with salt and took a big mouthful and then said, "Jesus! What's up with this fish?" Of course you can guess what had happened − Mum had mistaken Dad's soap powder for her flour and so we'd had well-soaped fish. We had a great laugh about that.

Funnily enough something similar had happened to my grandfather. He had been grumbling and shouting at my grandmother for something and came into the back kitchen to make his carry-out. My grandmother used yellow soap for washing and she always grated it so that it melted better and she had just grated a plateful when granddad came in to make his cheese and onion sandwiches. If he hadn't been so bad-tempered with her she might have told him he was using her soap, but as it was he went to work and handed his mate a soap and onion sandwich!

It was a happy place, Severn Street, with some nice shops handy for us on Beacon Lane, which, since we were at the bottom end of the street, was only three doors off. There was an old fashioned bakery where old Mr Morton made absolutely lovely bread, scones and potato cakes. I can still smell them when I think about the old days. Just opposite the bakery on the corner of White Street was a little shop which sold everything, sweets, newspapers, lemonade and groceries, run by a Mr Bacon, who only had one eye.

The only other shop I remember on Beacon Lane was Bibby's, and the thing I remember best about Bibby's was the big advertisement outside, showing a huge whale with a great big bottle of Bovril holding his jaws apart and a man lying on his tongue! I liked that advertisement when I was a lad. Opposite Bibby's there was a vegetable shop, so you could get most things on Beacon Lane.

There was loads of kids living around the area. I was in a gang with Eddie Fell, Frankie Walmsley, Freddy Brown, Norman and Lesley Brown, and George Bailey who was nicknamed Bala. We were little devils and used to catch flies and chuck them into spiders' webs, or collect daddy bunches* from underneath the window sills, put them in jamjars and release them in the house for devilment. My mother would batter me for that!

There were lots of games played, of course. When I was a little boy it was stuff like 'The farmer wants a wife', 'London Bridge is falling down', and so on, but when we were bigger it was Alalio* which meant a lot of running and chasing so was good fun.

We would run for miles, practically all around Everton, being chased. I wasn't keen on football, but as I got older I became quite a reasonable boxer and boxed at the Red Triangle.

I said I wasn't good at football, but I played it at least once, when the Venice Street head teacher saw me watching at a football tournament in Townsend Lane. One of our team hadn't turned up and Mr Snowdon, the Head, said I would have to stand in for the missing player. I was running around aimlessly by the opposition's goal mouth trying to keep out of the way and a lad called Georgie Savage kicked the ball and it hit me on the head. And it went into the goal! I had scored the opening goal and though it was a pure accident I was the hero of the day.

Like I said, I was never a great sportsman but I did like flying pigeons, which was a popular pastime in Everton at that time. There was one fellow called the Duke, he lived off Church Place, and he used to sell pigeons. But he'd trained them to fly to his home so you'd buy your bird, take it home and eventually fly it, and it would go straight back to the Duke, who would then sell it on to the next kid.

I got wise to this and bought a pigeon from him and then dyed its feathers. Then I went round to claim my bird back and there he was, with dye all over his hands, trying to get it off my pigeon. What was more, he used to lure other people's pigeons into his yard and then wring their necks and sell them to the Chinese for a bob apiece. Oh yes, he was a pretty naughty man on the quiet.

Next door to us on Severn Street lived a fireman, Mick Parry, and he had a great influence on me, because he played the guitar and sang and yodelled. He saw I was keen on music and actually made me my very first guitar, being good with his hands.

Schooldays

I went to St George's School, in Everton, opposite the library. Another boy who started when I did was Ronnie Diable; he was a real little villain, he screamed and attacked the teacher and ran out of the class room and all the way home to Northumberland Terrace. They chased him of course and brought him back to school, but he was very very strong willed. We used to get milk and a cob from Watts Bakery, and in the afternoon they gave us a pillow and we were supposed to have a nap. Ronnie and me usually kept all the others awake.

Once, my pal Tommy Hill and I went down Beacon Lane and ended up by Stanley Park and got lost. We were taken to a policeman who bought us some chips whilst he found out where we were from and after that we got 'lost' quite often, in order to get the chips... but we knew our way home really, of course.

It was in school that Mrs Thomas, one of the teachers, decided that she would try to teach any kids who were interested to play the accordion. My mother got one from Jacob Epstein's secondhand shop which was in Everton Valley opposite the Halfway House. She went down to buy a three piece suite but she bought the accordion, which was a bargain, as well. She gave it to my brother but unfortunately our Freddy was gammy-handed and had to hold the instrument upside down, which confused him and also poor Mrs Thomas, so he gave it up.

One day I was up in the bedroom, messing around, and I started to play the accordion and soon I was able to play quite well. I was lucky in that several members of my family were pretty good musicians so I took note of what they did and listened to their playing and this made things easier for me.

It wasn't only my family and our neighbour whose musical talents interested me, however; there was a busker who went around the pubs and played the guitar and sang. I never even knew his name but he had a great voice and I loved following him from pub to pub. He sang Jimmy Rogers songs, which I really liked, and he made me aware of music.

Peewit was another accordion playing busker who interested me, but he sang the same songs every Saturday night and always at breakneck speed so he could take his cap off and collect coppers. He was a great character and called all us lads 'son' and bought us packets of crisps from time to time.

Wartime

In 1939 Everton was crowded with shops, houses and people. When war was declared I remember a lad in my class whose father had joined up was given a badge and the brass buttons off his dad's overcoat.

I desperately wanted such things and was delighted when my own father was called up because now, I thought, I'd get brass buttons and so on. But I didn't realise they would take my dad away from us for over four years or I wouldn't have been so pleased.

Danger doesn't mean much to kids, so when we were in the air raid shelter with bombs whistling down and exploding deafeningly we were really made up by such massive bangs and we longed to go out each morning to collect shrapnel in dried milk tins. It was collected by the scrap metal people and melted down to make more bombs.

I was evacuated to Whitchurch some time around April 1941 but nothing much seemed to happen so my mother brought me home – just in time for the May blitz. Women had to work during the war because all the men were in the services – my mother was a clippie on the trams – so my grandmother brought us up.

The blitz was terrible for Everton, the library and the church were both badly damaged, all the windows of both were blown out – and the school was closed for a while. Next day I saw the coffins coming out of the houses, including those of children I had known. I remember one little girl I'd known being taken to the cemetery in a hearse drawn by black horses with black plumes on their heads.

I had a narrow escape one morning when I'd been out collecting shrapnel from the previous night's raid. Me and our Freddy and our Jake went up to a piece of ground opposite the library which had been flattened out in order to make it into an emergency water supply. When we got there, we found a great big mound as if someone had been digging there, so we climbed up and looked down into the hole and we saw the fins of a massive bomb sticking out.

We got down into the hole, thinking that we would clean all the soil off the bomb, and whilst we were at it a voice said, "Christ almighty! There's a gang of kids down there!" This fellow had climbed the mound as we had to see what had caused the damage and was none too pleased to find it occupied! The men soon had us out of the hole and chased us away but we hung around whilst they cordoned the area off and then the bomb disposal squad arrived and defused the bomb. The soldiers who did the work were congratulated and all the young girls flirted with them and someone brought them whisky and sandwiches.

Then there was the Sunday morning when we'd got up early to go fishing. We were on the west side of St George's Church and were looking down over the river when a tremendous explosion occurred. Apparently it was a ship called the *Malakand* which blew up in the Huskisson dock, causing enormous and very costly damage. That scene has stayed in my memory for many years.

One adventure we had was in St Domingo's Road, in a row of small shops with houses above them. One of the shops had been occupied by an Irish chap, who left suddenly, and a group of us boys got into the now empty shop and found a revolver and some ammunition, sticks of dynamite, all sorts. We were questioned by the police, of course, but they didn't tell us anything and we never did find out any real details, though now I suppose that it was either a German spy or possibly an IRA terrorist. Fortunately for us we couldn't get the ammunition into the revolver, though we tried!

As I grew older, music became more and more important to me, and also I was very keen on reading. I loved the Everton library and went there often to get books for myself, my mum, my dad and the rest of the family. But the best thing about the library were the sort of alcoves on either side of the main doors. In the evenings, when it was cold and wet, we lads used to poke a stick through and open the gates. Then we would get into the shelter with our guitars and other instruments and play country music to our hearts content.

When the police came they wouldn't chase us out because we were doing no harm, we weren't near the pub, we weren't wandering the streets causing trouble, in fact because of the resonance and echo of the library alcoves, our singing and playing resulted in a truly excellent sound. So you can see I remember the library – those were great days. And it was from days like that that my music evolved, though I never thought when we were crammed into those alcoves, that one day I would make a living by playing music.

* see glossary

Elizabeth Murphy

I was born at N°80 Everton Road on November 22nd 1919. It was a tall old house with attics and cellars which was in the block between Cresswell Street and Queens Road. N°78 was the Royal public house, N°82 a small shop and N°84 the Masonic Arms, always known as Maybury's.

My paternal grandmother and aunts lived in 52 Cresswell Street opposite the playground of Steers Street School. These houses had small gardens and a path and three steps to the front door. They had bay windows draped with Nottingham lace curtains, with an aspidistra plant on a stand in the centre of the window.

When I was three years old my grandmother died and we moved to Molyneaux Road, Kensington. My elder sister had started school at St. Francis Xaviers so when I was five I accompanied her there. It was too long a journey to come home for lunch so we went to my aunt's house in Cresswell St. I recall standing at her gate one day when a herd of cows was being driven up Cresswell Street towards the Abbatoir. One poor creature pushed open the gate next door and walked up the path so I beat a hasty retreat! Another day I stood with my aunt and sister watching the R101 pass overhead. "I don't believe in those things," a neighbour said, "if God had intended us to fly He would have given us wings." I thought she was right, especially when the airship was involved in tragedy.

We had little time to stand and stare on our way to school but I enjoyed the journey home, especially after my sister moved on to Grammar School and I made the journey alone. There were so many interesting things and people to see. One was an old lady known as Teapot Mary, who wore a teacosy on her head and carried various utensils on a rope around her waist. All her worldly goods were carried in brown paper carrier bags or parcels. Nowadays she would be known as a bag lady.

A small legless man propelled himself around by his hands while sitting on a wooden platform on four small wheels. I think he sold newspapers for a living.

At lunchtime we walked along Shaw Street, up steep Eastbourne Street, then Plumpton Street across Everton Road to Cresswell Street. There were common lodging houses for homeless men on one side of Shaw Street. One had a board in the window saying 'Good clean beds 6p per night'. On the other side of Shaw Street was a small park where the War Memorial stood and sandstone had been excavated at one time. We enjoyed scrambling round the quarry, feeling like mountaineers, although it was probably quite small. Miss Tully's sweetshop was at the bottom of Eastbourne Street, where we bought Fairy Whispers and licorice bootlaces. The houses in Plumpton Street had cellar kitchens and many had a table in the window. I hated but could not resist looking through the area railing at one house where a fly encrusted flypaper hung above an open tin of condensed milk.

We also bought sweets at a small shop which was beneath the landing of houses above. Toffee balls and cinnamon balls. Ariel Gray's warehouse was on the opposite side of Everton Road. It had evidently been built over the graveyard of the Fabius Chapel and tombstones lined the walls around it. They were very old, mainly eighteenth century and the long 'S' was used in the inscriptions.

I visited my aunt after Sunday School but Cresswell Street was very different then. Steers Street School was closed and a deadly quiet lay on the street. I was warned by my aunt not to bounce a ball or raise my voice but I would not have dared. My childless aunt and uncle (a master printer) lived comfortable lives and so did their neighbours but there was great poverty near to St. Francis Xaviers School at this time.

Many of the children wore police clothes and clogs, made so that they could not be pawned, and even many who wore their own clothes were undernourished. Miss Crangle, an inspiring teacher and a compassionate woman often discreetly sent me, as a monitor, to buy barmcakes and milk from a nearby Transport Cafe for the malnourished children she taught. 'Good old days'? Not for these children and their parents.

Ann Cunningham

When my mother-in-law was younger she and her husband and their three sons were very hard up, particularly as her husband gave his mother half his wage even after his marriage. So when Leslie, her middle son, found a pet rabbit and brought it home, her first thought was that it would make a nice meal. But the children started screaming and when she went out to the yard to do the foul deed the rabbit had disappeared. She always imagined that someone else had made a dinner out of it.

My husband Freddie remembers the days when you always wore hand-me-downs, kids were always waddling around in wellies several sizes too large. One one occasion the nurse appeared at school unexpectedly, and one of the boys was wearing his dad's vest, which came right down to his feet and had to be rolled up round his waist and stuffed into his underpants.

Realising that when the nurse made him undress he would be a laughing stock he climbed over the school wall and hid in the back entry until the bell went for dinner, and the nurse, presumably, had moved on.

My Mother's Story

Some of my childhood memories of Everton are around Havelock Street. It was one of the streets that was so steep that it had a railing all the way to the bottom. As children we played and tossed on the railings.

The women used to congregate in Heyworth Street with hand barrows wearing Mary-Ellen shawls selling fruit and veg. The market in Casaneau Street sold household goods and second hand clothes, not so much food stuff. It was lit by naphtha lamps. Men used to juggle plates, but they never broke any, it was just to attract attention This market had a merry go round of small 'Bobby Horses' as they were called. They sold mock toffee apples for lp with a ride on the Bobby Horses. They sold stick jaw toffee which did stick your jaws together and 'lucky mines' a piece of toffee, which if you were lucky enough had a coin inside it.

On warm nights all the kids played together with two mothers turning a skipping rope from one side of the street to another. Often the adults pushed a piano onto the street for a special occasion and they would congregate and sing. If you had a piano you were 'well off'!

Whatmoughs, the local dairy sold fresh milk. We used to go every day. They served it from a churn with a long handled dipper in a measured half or one pint. They also sold ice cream, homemade and dished out in tubs made from very thin wood, rather like strawberry punnet wood, bent into a circle. The ice cream had the top flattened off and a lid put on.

On Bank Holidays we used to go on outings to nearby beauty spots, to Sefton Meadow, or Ford by charabanc.

Home Life

Our house was lit by gas mantles which you could poke your match through very easily. Monday, of course, was washday – most people washed on a Monday. The clothes were boiled in the copper, then rinsed, then 'blued' with a dolly blue – they were starched with home made starch, flour and water made into a jelly with boiling water. Everyone kept their step clean and the children were given a coarse apron and a sandstone piece which ground more sandstone into a powder to grind over the sandstone step. A finishing touch was the bevelled edge put around the step with the sandstone – the surrounding paving stones were kept spotless as well.

Once a year my Gran bought a packet of 'lime', a dolly blue and a tallow candle, this was mixed together. The lime melted everything else into an emulsion which was snow-white, but burnt the skin. This was painted onto the yard walls and the outside toilet with a yard brush. Gran was kitted out in a turban around her head for this event. Bundles of wooden chips were sold for the coal fire which included an oven at the side of the fire which cooked everything, although we had a small gas cooker.

Any rubbish was burnt on it, and it was damped down at night by Gran who used to pile potato peelings and cold cinders onto the fire, this prevented flames from bursting out and kept the heat in the grate for long into the night. The whole grate was black leaded, a block of black lead was moistened and applied. This when dried was polished – a daily job. The kettle, large and black was perpetually on the fire, this was black leaded as well.

The War

The war was the great catalyst, we were bombed out and we had to leave our most treasured possessions behind, granddad's camphor wood chest which he had brought home from the sea.

I joined the forces and people were scattered, whole streets and families gone due to the bombing. I remember men didn't come home to the women they had left behind. The women had taken employment in the factories or had gone into the forces. Their life was different.

During the war we were re-housed into a requisitioned house, but after the war we were re-housed in Speke, but my happy vivid memories of a childhood spent in Everton remain.

Mrs Florence Jones

The holidays were over and the term had begun. Children of all ages were on their way to school. And so was I. Stepping out of the door holding my mother's hand, I was dressed in a dark dress with a white starched pinafore over it, a long coat, and button boots on my feet.

Up and down our street, doors slammed and children screamed. The school I should have gone to, Venice Street Infants, had been taken over for wounded prisoners of war, though people were so hostile about them that the German prisoners had to be sent elsewhere and it was our own wounded soldiers who were now housed in the school.

Walking down the street, we met Lily and her mother. This was her first morning as well. I knew Lily by sight but she was never allowed to play out with us.

Granton Road School reminded me of a prison with its high walls and a huge clanging bell in the thick wooden door. We sang a song in time with the bell: *"Come to school don't be late, bring your pencil and your slate."*

Lily and I were taken to the babies' class. We gave our names. "Lily Broderick", and "Florence Louise Titherington". We sat in baby chairs with round backs. In the big grate, the fire had a guard around it.

We played with sand-trays and shells. Some of the children had to be taken home because they were crying so much. They were the 'one family' children – 'only children' as we'd call them nowadays – and there weren't many of them then.

At home, nobody asked whether I liked being at school. You just had to get on with it. No hugs, no kisses. Children had to be seen but not heard. After school, Edie collected me. "Shall we go and see if the old ladies have put anything out?" she said.

A few doors down the street, a mother and daughter lived. Every so often, they cleared the house and put things they didn't want any longer on the back step for children to take. Edie always took the bric-a-brac while I took the books.

I love cats and when ours died and we didn't get another one, I did my best to replace it. Whenever I saw a cat I'd try to make it follow me home. "Here she is with another cat," one of the boys would say, chasing the poor thing away.

But I never stopped trying until one day, a big cat that I'd brought home managed to get into the meat safe in the yard and feasted on the weekend joint. I had to take the cat back to where

I'd found it, but it kept following me back again. Eventually I managed to lose it and was warned never to bring another cat home.

We did get a cat though – because we had a mouse take up residence in the back kitchen. We already had a dog. The people next door had a parrot. They used to put it out on the wall next to our shed. It was always saying, "Time to get up, Harry!" A few people had parrots which they generally kept in cages hung by the front door. On their way to school, children would stand underneath saying, "Hello Polly!" This sometimes made them late for school as the huge door was locked promptly at nine o'clock.

After a morning at Granton Road School, we'd usually go home to a plate of boiled rice with sultanas in it. In the afternoon, we had our lessons in the Anfield Weslyan Church. The children who had been there in the morning went to school in the afternoon. This went on until the end of the war when the wounded soldiers were moved out and we got our Venice Street School back.

On our way to the church, we passed the football ground, where goats belonging to the cowkeeper grazed on the grassy slope at the back of the Kop.

On Duck Apple Night – or Halloween as it's called nowadays – the boys had a great time rigging up a line with apples tied to it at regular intervals. Blindfolded and with our hands behind our backs we had to try and bite an apple, though sometimes it was a piece of soap we bit on that the boys had tied on secretly and guided into our mouths. Then it was time to duck for apples bobbing about in a bowl of water. Halloween was Edie's birthday and she always got the biggest apple father could find. Then we had to tidy up and go to bed.

Even when we were older, we had to go to bed at ten o'clock. If we were talking too much in bed, father would shout upstairs, "Pack up there." Under our breath we'd say cheekily, "We have no bag," and giggle hysterically, although we'd said it so often before.

As Lily and I were both able to read, we were moved out of the babies' class and we became firm friends, going to school and coming home together. One day on the way home, we met some of the boys. They didn't like ro be seen talking to girls, but didn't mind playing with them to make up a team.

"Playing rounders tonight?" Tommy called.

"Yes," I said. But Lily wasn't allowed to play in the street. Tommy was the only one with a bat and ball and the game finished when he was called in. We had to be careful not to offend him or he'd take the bat in. We played at the bottom of our street. One side was a brick wall and the other a long entrance to the shippen. 'Fagging' – or fielding – across the main road it was quite safe as there was very little traffic and what there was you heard coming while it was still a long way off.

On dark nights, we played guessing outside the brightly lit sweet shop windows until we were called in for bed.

"School in the morning," father would say.

"I haven't got to go," Edie protested.

"You will soon, and you need your beauty sleep."

It was no use lingering because we had to be asleep in the single bed in our parents' room by the time they came to bed. We used to do all kinds of tricks like standing on our heads to see how far we could get up the wall until we heard their footsteps on the stairs, then we'd scramble under the blankets pretending to be asleep.

There was a text hanging on the wall, '*Thou God seest me*', which was pointed out to us when we misbehaved.

One day we managed to get hold of a box of Phulnana face powder and plastered our faces with it then went to sleep, to be awakened by the horrified voice of my mother saying, "My God, what's the matter with these children?"

There was a walk-in cupboard under the stairs and we spent a lot of time in it. We used to dress up and entertain the family by acting out nursery rhymes. This one time I had a brilliant idea. I persuaded Edie to be the cow and to fill her mouth with water and spit it out as I milked her. It shocked our parents and we were sent to bed.

"I told you I didn't want to be the cow," Edie grumbled.

"Oh, shut up and go to sleep."

Queenie, our oldest sister, slept in the middle room with Dolly, the next one. When Queenie got married, Edie and I moved in with Dolly. It was terrible! The other two were fatter than me and lying between them I felt like the slice of meat in a sandwich. The bed was always lumpy, and I was always complaining.

Dolly said, "For Heaven's sake, shut up! You're like the princess who slept on a pea."

In the parlour there was an American organ and a piano which we couldn't touch. We were only allowed in the parlour when visitors came. There wasn't much room in there, what with the green plush suite and chairs to match. On the mantelpiece were two marley horses flanked by white marble figures in glass cases. A corner cupboard held some fascinating things, the best of which was the glass walking stick with a cork in the handle, filled with those brightly coloured sweets called 'hundreds and thousands'.

"I dare you to take the cork out," Edie said. "You do it," I told her. But we never did, fearing the consequences.

When a rich uncle, aunt and cousin came at night, we had to go in the parlour. They left their fur coats on the chair and we used to try them on, taking care to put them back in the same position afterwards. "I hope they give us some money," Edie said. And they did! They gave us a whole shilling. Twelve pennies. It was like a fortune to us. We couldn't spend it all at once, we had to save some of it.

One of our daytime visitors the boys called 'Sweet Muchacha'. She wore a feather boa and when she tossed it over her shoulder and said, "Have you heard about ..." Mother would say, "Go and play in the yard. Little pitchers have big ears!" So we never heard anything, although we tried our best. Another visitor was a very tall women who wore a hat like a plant pot and a black knitted shawl and big boots. The boys called her 'Fairy Flannel Feet'. She wasn't married and kept house for a doctor.

When we had visitors for tea we had to play in the yard until they'd finished, hoping they'd leave enough for us. My father was very particular about manners. "No elbows on the table." "Sit up straight, don't lounge!"

We were not allowed to buy comics, although we read other people's, hiding them when father was in. Also, he didn't like anybody banging up against his chair when he was sitting in it. He never went to a dentist. When a tooth ached he used a penknife and, leaning on the arm of an upright chair, would eventually dig it out. Our chairs were upright too. The long bench which we sat on at mealtimes made us sit properly.

The big dresser had drawers in the front which were supposed to be for scarves and gloves but were actually stuffed with string and wool and sewing cotton which all got tangled up. When it got to the stage that the drawer would no longer shut, mam used to spread a newspaper on the floor, turn the drawer upside down on it and say, "All collect what you want and the rest will go in the bin."

Then there was a scramble to pick out things we thought we needed before mother threw them out. There were always the same things that went back into the drawer time and time again.

An epidemic of diphtheria affected many of the children in our street. Edie was one of them. She was taken to hospital, then men from the Corporation came and sprayed every room in the house with disinfectant, leaving it all smelly and damp. I had to stay away from school for fear of infection.

As the only telephone available was the Undertaker's, we had to go there and ring the hospital. I can still remember my mother saying the number, "Old Swan 78". Some of the children who were taken to hospital with diphtheria never came back.

Extract from 'Memoirs of a Liverpool Stripper'
by Flo Jones

Mrs J Spruce

The Everton I remember so well was the vibrant busy district of the 1930's up to 1955 before the reluctant exodus to Kirkby, due to redevelopment of the area.

I attended Everton Terrace and Roscommon Schools. Everton Terrace School was very distinctive, perched high on St George's Hill, with its two tiered schoolyards. There were school rooms on three floors, with never-ending stairs!

In the basement there were hot water showers, the stalls hewn out of the red sandstone that was the natural strata of Everton. Friday mornings, equipped with soap and towel, the children would enjoy the luxury of it.

There were very few houses with bathrooms then, I personally knew of no-one with a bathroom. We were also told there was a well on the premises.

The second most important place in my life was the Weslyan Church in Great Homer Street. It was a thriving church with a strong congregation, Girl Guides, youth clubs and a Mother's Meeting. The Rydal youth club was also based there, run by Edgar Bibby of Bibby's Mills. Commander Bibby of the Fleet Air Arm was quite a war hero

The Rydal club was supported by the Rydal Public School of which Mr Bibby was an old boy. I was a member of this club, it opened up a whole new world to us – with skiing holidays, which were unheard of in those early post-war years – plus camping and London weekends. Mr Bibby also opened many doors for youngsters seeking employment.

The other major club was Shrewsbury House, which was again supported by the Public School of the same name. This one however, was strictly for boys.

The Orange Lodge played a big part in our lives. Every street seemed to have their own Lodge, vain in its dresses and street decorations. We had organised outings and dances. The eve of 12th July was spent walking along the length of Netherfield Road viewing the decorated streets.

On the great day itself the schools were devoid of pupils. After a day out in Southport there would be one long party in the streets that would last until the early hours of the morning.

Netherfield Road wash-house was the hub of activity with every mother taking her washing. Looking for one's mother through clouds of steam was an adventure! Then there was the queueing up for the slipper baths in the basement – we may have been poor, but we were certainly clean! These were happy days when families lived in close proximity. People seemed to marry people they grew up with, and settled near to mum.

As a child of the 1930's my earliest memory is of lying snug in my bed in Abram Street, with the gas light flickering, listening to the rattle of the trams and the sound of people's voices as they were emptying out of the pubs. But best of all, my dad's tram driver's overcoat on my bed, smelling of tobacco and warmth.

All was well in my little world.

A Dip into the Past
FB McCann

The area of Everton in which I was reared was a poor district of Liverpool, with two-up and two-down, back-to-back houses roofed with sombre grey slates. Indoor plumbing was restricted to a solitary cold water tap which constantly dripped into a badly chipped brown stone sink situated in a gloomy back kitchen.

Sunlight never permeated into this room due to the close proximity of the house next door. The lavatory was to be found at the bottom of a narrow yard, in which one did not remain longer than was necessary in the winter time, and which would freeze into solid ice in sever conditions. The area no longer exists, thankfully, having been turned into a park.

Poverty I grew up with, and accepted, because everyone was in the same position. Unemployment was exceptionally high in the early 1930's. The children of my neighbourhood were mostly undernourished, badly clothed and lacked decent footwear. Thick cardboard, roughly cut to fit sandals or pumps, was used as an inner-sole to keep out the cold and the damp.

To quote a hackneyed expression, "I endured more beatings than hot dinners", which just about sums up a loveless upbringing by my old grandmother; my mother remarried two years after my father died and moved in wit her new in-laws. The one thing that readily comes to mind now is that it made me bitter, and oblivious to the suffering of others. Also, it bred in me a great determination to climb out of this existence by any means possible.

Two aunts also resided with my grandmother and I, they both had menial factory jobs earning very low wages. At an early age the terms 'laid off' or 'short time' held an ominous significance in a household that was always struggling to survive.

Taking in washing was a means to augment the weekly budget. The drudgery that this work entailed had to be experienced to be fully appreciated. For my part, the collection and delivery was my contribution. Two collections were made on the way home from school at lunchtime, two more before I returned. The remaining three were completed after 4pm when school finished for the day. So ended Monday.

Tuesday was like living in a perpetual warm cloying fog of never-ending steam from the copper boiler in the back kitchen, heated by a small coal fire which greedily devoured the liberal shovelfuls of small shiny black nuts. Rinsing the whites in cold blue water before transferring them to the wringing machine. I hated this contraption wholeheartedly, and the interminable hours spent turning the handle that turned the rollers which forced the water from the clothes. Oh, how my one good arm ached after this operation!

Wednesday was drying day. Fine weather was a bonus because the washing could be pegged out on the line in the backyard. If the weather was inclement then every inch of space was utilised. Two racks were used, one in the living quarters and the second above the stairway on the upstairs landing.

The drying racks consisted of four long poles raised and lowered by rope and pulley. Blankets, sheets, pillow cases and a variety of personal linens were crammed onto these. Smaller items were suspended around the fireplace, either on the brass rail or on the fireguard itself. The smell from the damp clothing assailed your nostrils wherever you were in the tiny house.

Wednesday evening my two aunts, after working at their respective jobs during the day, tackled the pressing and the ironing. Two flat irons were used, heated on the gas ring alternately. They would spit on them to teat the temperature by the sizzling noise it made. They moved like automatons, and when it was completed they were completely exhausted by their efforts. Neat piles grew on the chairs and the sideboard, representing each individual customer.

Their final task was to wrap the seven parcels in brown paper ready for me to deliver the next day.

Mrs Southern was my first customer, a kindly old soul with features reminiscent of a Dresden figurine. She always fussed over me, asking how I was, had I seen my mother lately and was I doing well at school? I answered her enquiries truthfully and politely whilst she wrapped two shillings in a small brown envelope and solemnly advised me to keep it safe for my grandmother.

A pitiful sum, but in those far off days it would feed us for at least two days, as food was cheap and plentiful. My reward was always the same each week — the previous week's issue of two boys' books, namely the 'Adventure' and the 'Wizard' which, contained in them were stories that would gladden any youngster's heart. Cheap rubbish they may have been, but in hindsight some of the space stories have come true in my lifetime. To say I devoured their contnts was an understatement, for I was an avid reader.

Mrs Williamson was my next call before returning to school in the afternoon. She wanted her washing done by someone else but resented paying for it, counting out the coins one by one grudgingly at the back entry door. Never once did I enter her house (perhaps to her I was a common little boy). My reward was two pennied at Christmas time wrapped in gaily coloured paper and tied with tinsel.

Mrs Harrison I called on after school was finished for the day.

It was imperative that the washing was delivered before her twin daughters reached home, for if I didn't achieve this my life was made miserable. The children were cruel and callous with their remarks to me.

To them I was a figure to poke fun at for their twisted sense of humour. In their superior tone they would enquire as to why my hair was un-parted, where was my raincoat or wellies if it was wet? Did I enjoy being small? When I stammered and blushed to the roots of my carroty hair they were in their element. My deformed left arm was a butt of their taunts.

When I left this house there were tears of indignation and frustration coursing down my cheeks. No doubt it was my introduction to the class system, because as a servant I was beneath their consideration. The penny given as a reward I could willingly have forgone in exchange for some kind words in that household.

In contrast, a visit to Mrs Davidson was a welcome relief. The aroma of cooking and baking smells made my mouth water when I entered her home. Her husband was always in a wheelchair situated close to the window, to enable him to watch the world go by. He was always surrounded by newspapers and books. A tragic accident at work had left him paralysed from the waist down. Strangely, he was always cheerful when I was there.

Compensation and a pension for life had left them fairly comfortably well off in comparison to the majority in that area. His wife was an industrious type of person, only happy when her hands were busily engaged in the hundred and one mundane tasks a home and a crippled spouse produced. She was always singing and whistling merrily, maybe it was infectious but my spirits were always higher when I departed from them. A packet od sweets and two sweet scones was my reward.

The local moneylender, Mrs Foster, was the next client. A brass plate that was burnished like gold was firmly fixed to her front door depicting the nature of her business. On receipt of her clean washing she would meticulously examine each item before tendering the half crown charge. Borrowers were always received at the back of the house and repayments were also made there.

An exorbitant interest rate was levied on every loan, in the region of 20% to the poor unfortunates who were in arrears, preferably in a crowded shop or thoroughfare. The person concerned would slink off in utter dejection, confused and shamefaced to her home. She was most certainly not my favourite person, I likened her to a leech, especially her clammy and sticky hands.

With the usual warning ringing in my ears not to enter the Widow Brown's house I used to quickly knock at the scullery door to be opened by a rather untidy, frumpish woman. Her age would be about 40 years, most noticeable was the gin-soaked breath and the obnoxious stench of cheap perfume, that exuded from her person.

It was reputed that she regularly had nocturnal visits from the opposite sex who left surreptitiously before dawn. I often went on the odd errand for her when it was required, usually for two ounces of boiled ham and a quarter pound of inexpensive margarine from the Co-Op. Her attitude to me was always courteous and pleasant. Besides, a halfpenny always came in useful, so what right did I have to cast the first stone?

Last but not least was Mrs Hitchens. Never come before 8pm were my instructions, as her husband was not to be disturbed until he had completed his evening meal, enjoyed his pipe and read the evening paper. He was an office manager in the Liverpool Cotton Exchange and his word was law at work and at home.

Pompous and self-centred was my silent appraisal of his character. His wife pandered to his every need, fawning over him as though he was King George V himself, without complaint. They had two sons who were both attending College and were as overbearing as their father towards their mothers.

I cannot recollect a kind word or gesture being directed towards the hen-pecked, nervous softly spoken lady, during my visits to the house. Whilst collecting her dirty washing during a very severe winter spell I was given a carrier bag containing some of her younger boys' clothes. "Don't be annoyed," she had whispered hesitantly, "they will keep you warm and dry on your rounds."

I knew my grandmother would not respond kindly to charity of this nature. I was in a dilemma. Firstly, I could not just hurt this kind lady's feelings, and secondly, the reception at home would be against acceptance of cast-offs. Fortunately for me, my youngest aunt was in the house when I returned and she inspected the clothing while I just stood and listened to the tirade of abuse from my guardian. I was never right whatever I did, it seemed.

Physical punishment at home always consisted of being boxed heavily around the head or liberal doses of the cane around the legs or forearms. One thing it taught me was how to duck and avoid any real damage to my person. My aunt resolved the situation that the clothing was in good condition and she personally would shorten the blue gabardine mackintosh and hem and insert some darts in the grey shorts. A pair of well worn football boots had been included, and, although too large, were the first I had ever owned.

Thursday ended with an early departure to bed clutching my precious books and a few sweets. By disciplining oneself to suck slowly and then resisting the temptation to chew or bite, you savoured the flavour much longer. (I still find myself doing that to this day – old habits die hard).

By turning up the paraffin oil lamp a little higher I could read in comfort, and was soon lost in the fictitious yarns of my paper heroes. Often I heard a heavy tread on the staircase signifying my grandmother was on her way up to bed. Hurriedly my treasured books were placed under the pillow, out of sight but not out of mind.

Life was not all doom and gloom, for I was involved in various activities outside the home. Representing my school at football, cricket and English baseball was an achievement for an undersized puny boy of nine years of age. How I remember seeing my name printed in heavy Germanic script on the team sheet for the first time. A deep sense of pride brought a lump to my throat and a sensation of happiness I had never experienced before. The number of times I passed the School notice board just to see again, my name, was incalculable.

Sunday School opened up a new and exciting episode in my young life, for it was there I had the good fortune to meet a young male teacher – Mr Godwin. He was a product of the old Seaman's Orphanage. A time-served electrical engineer employed by Cammel Lairds Shipyards. This young man who by word and deed epitomised Christianity. Five scruffy, underprivileged boys he took under his wing, and every four weeks on a Saturday afternoon he organised excursions to venues we had never known existed.

Thurstaston was a favourite place to visit, for through him we learned local history, the fauna and the flora, and exciting climbs up the sandstone rocks, from which we could view the mighty Welsh hills and tiny boats sailing on the River Dee beneath us. On rainy days we would visit Liverpool's own Museum or Art Gallery, to be educated in such a way that it was enjoyable.

Other interesting places were the grave of the Child of Hale, Liverpool Airport, Ship Building in Birkenhead, Chester Cathedral amongst a host of others too numerous to mention.

Sadly, this man died as he lived, for in 1940 a scratch crew was required for the *SS Lancastria* and of course, he offered his services. The ill-fated vessel was sunk off Dunkirk by German bombers during the evacuation with tremendous loss of life. On hearing of his death months later I felt as though I had lost a dear friend or close relative.

Realising now when I look back to over fifty years ago, one thing seems crystal clear to me – that the harsh and unyielding upbringing which I endured in those long dark days, that poverty and hunger were to be beaten only by one's own endeavours.

Seeing my wife loading her automatic washing machine and pressing the required programme often takes me back in time.

The good old days – there weren't many!

Glossary

Amami Night   Named after a brand of shampoo popular at the time. It refers to the common practice among girls of washing their hair on a Friday night prior to the weekend's entertainment

Bob   A shilling in pre-decimal money (5p)

Cherry-wobs   Cherry stones used in a childrens' game

Cobbling   Shoe repairing

Coolies   Chinese galley staff, frequently employed on ships of the time

Daddy Bunches   Daddy-long-legs (crane flies)

Euialio/Alalio Relievo/il-ally-o	A childrens' game, popular until the 1950's
Fender	A low metal frame to confine burning coals to the hearth
Gentian Violet	An antiseptic
Half a Crown	Two shillings and sixpence in pre-decimal currency (14½p)
Housy-housy	Bingo (a game)
Ollies	Marbles
Ritual Baths	Jewish religious observances
ROE	Royal Ordnance Factories
Shippon	Many dairy cattle were kept in buildings within towns, and their milk sold directly to customers
Snobbing	Shoe making or repairing
Steerage	The cheapest passenger accommodation